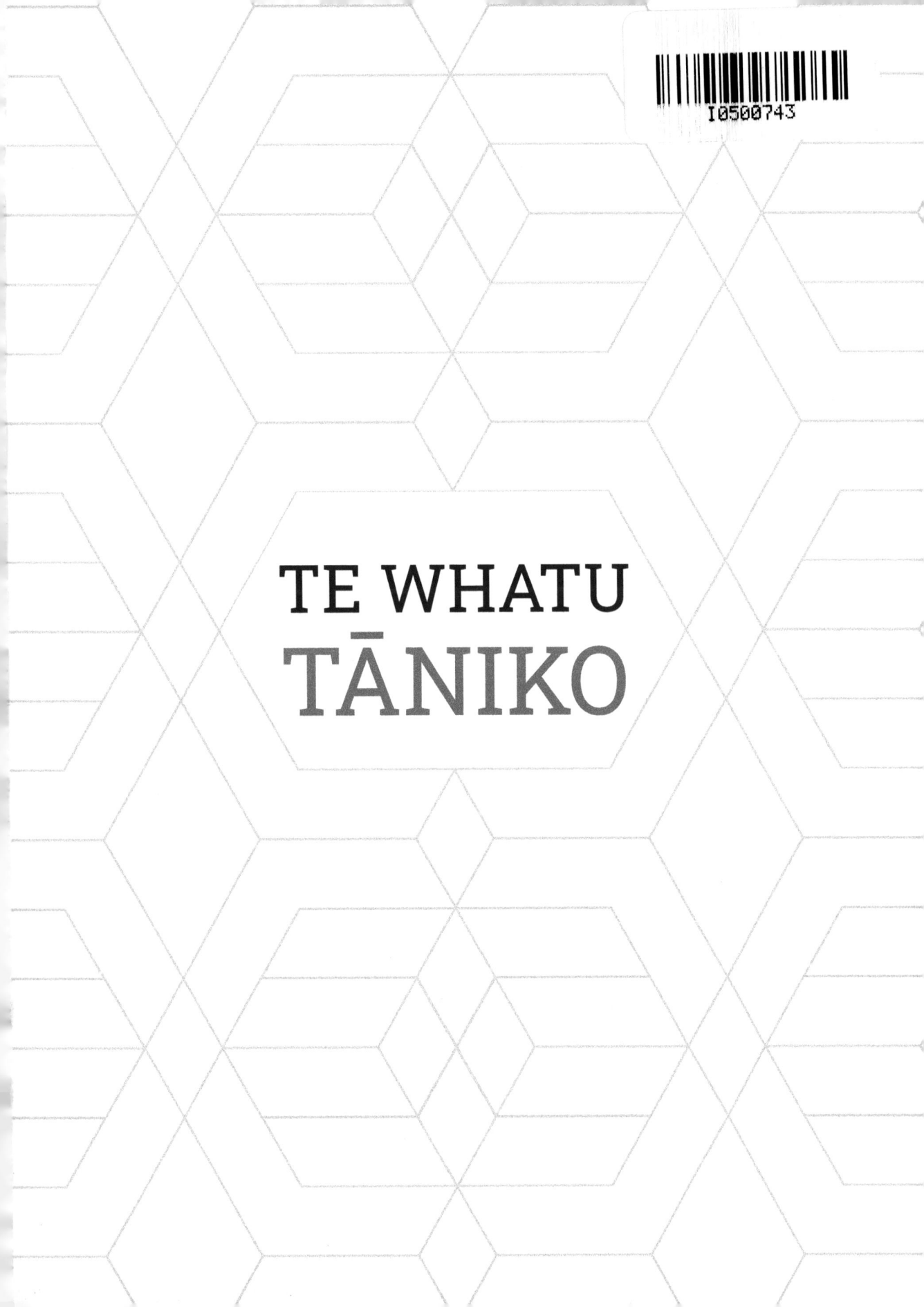

TE WHATU
TĀNIKO

Also by Hirini Mead

Magnificent Te Maori

Māori Art on the World Scene

Ngā Pepeha a Ngā Tūpuna

Tawhaki: The Deeds of a Demi God

Tawhaki-nui-a Hema

Te Taniwha o Tuara-rangaia

The Taniwha of Tuara-rangaia

Te Toi Whakairo: The Art of Maori Carving

The People of the Land

Tikanga Māori: Living by Māori Values

We Speak Maori

TE WHATU TĀNIKO

TĀNIKO WEAVING: TECHNIQUE AND TRADITION

Hirini Moko Mead

Oratia

Ki taku tamāhine ki a
Linda Tuhiwai Te Rina Smith

Published by Oratia Books, Oratia Media Ltd, 783 West Coast Road, Oratia, Auckland 0604, New Zealand (www.oratia.co.nz).

ISBN 978-0-947506-61-2

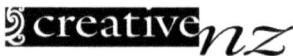

The publisher acknowledges the generous support of Creative New Zealand for this publication.

Cover image: Korowai woven from muka and feathers of the spotted kiwi by Dame Rangimarie Hetet for her eldest child Charles Wilson Hetet over 90 years ago. Collection of the Hetet Whanau; photograph by Len Hetet

First published 1968 as *Te Whatu Taaniko*
Reprinted 1973, 1987
Second edition as *Te Whatu Tāniko* 1999
Reprinted 2006
This edition 2019
Reprinted 2021, 2024

Contents

Preface 6

Preface to the 2019 edition..9

1 An Introduction to Māori Costume...11

2 The Tāniko Weaving Technique..19

3 The Discovery of the Tāniko Technique... 30

4 The History and Development of Tāniko Weaving 36

5 Style and Tāniko Patterns... 59

6 The Classification of Tāniko Patterns 71

7 General Conclusions.. 94

8 Instructions for Learning Tāniko Weaving................................. 99

Glossary of Māori words...127

Bibliography... 131

Index...133

Preface

Kua tō te rā, kua whiti te rā hou. (The sun has set and a new sun has risen.) Earlier editions of this book have, like the sun, set into an abyss of darkness, and with the dawning of a new day a revised version emerges. *Taniko Weaving* first appeared in 1952 and then in 1968 it was rewritten and redesigned under the Reed label. While the main text retains its usefulness, parts have been left behind by the changing dictates of fashion and by the fact the Māori world has changed.

Māori costume is firmly established among all Māori communities throughout the nation. Wherever Māori groups present action songs, poi dances, stick games and men's haka (war dance) they will be seen dressed in what has become appropriate and necessary costume. The basic costume has not changed since 1968. What has changed is the length of the underskirt for women and the length of the piupiu (dancing skirt) which rises and falls according to overseas fluctuations in skirt lengths. In male costume there has been an increasing acceptance of the maro (apron) which has been redesigned to look like shorts with front and back flaps. This new item is practical and effectively replaces the piupiu for men.

The piupiu itself continues to be of prime importance for women because of the swishing sound it makes, and because it emphasises the swaying of the body. In some groups the belt band in men's piupiu has widened and this is covered with tāniko patterns. Without this item of costume a performance loses much of its visual impact.

An obligatory part of the piupiu is an underskirt (panekoti). This may be red or black, which are highly favoured colours, or may be some other colour that is significant to a school group or sports team. Tāniko borders are often added to the underskirt.

Women continue to be covered above the waist with a bodice which at the present time is almost invariably made using tapestry weave, not the tāniko technique. In 1968 tapestry was becoming the favoured way of producing tāniko patterns. Twenty years later it had not been supplanted either by a return to the more traditional method of tāniko or by some new and faster technique as might have been expected. Instead, its use had become almost universal. By 1996, however, there was evidence of other techniques being used, the outstanding one being silk screening.

An interesting modern development is the adoption of new bone pendants as part of Māori costume. Two decades ago it was rare to find any performing teams wearing bone hei (neck pendants). Interest was focused mainly upon the greenstone heitiki or on plastic versions of it. While interest in the greenstone tiki remains strong, bone hei made of cow bone or whalebone have become acceptable. Part of the reason for greater acceptance is their general popularity in New Zealand society today. Bone hei are worn by Māori people from all walks of life and by an increasing number of Pākehā citizens. Another important reason is their price: they are far cheaper than a greenstone tiki and infinitely preferable to a plastic one. Today it is no longer unusual to find every member of a cultural group wearing a bone hei.

Another interesting change is the development in male costume of better ways of applying moko (tattoo) to the face. Earlier, many groups applied facial moko with artless abandon producing patterns which were merely squiggly lines. Now many groups have found useful techniques and aids to produce patterns which are more convincing as moko and which are more beautiful. The film industry has helped find quicker ways of applying moko and some of its know-how is being adopted by several cultural teams.

It is worth noting that weavers overseas have taken an interest in tāniko weaving, which is a form of finger weaving. Our indigenous technique of producing decorative bands is a contribution to the world of weaving and it adds to the wealth of weaving techniques that are available to modern weavers. Tāniko weaving has not really become popular in New Zealand, nor has it died out either. To ensure its survival the modern weaver must be prepared to explore the technique's potential more fully than in the past, with the aim of ensuring tāniko becomes not only easier to do but also produces a more interesting result that still preserves the main shape of tāniko patterns. Another possibility is for someone to invent a computerised machine that does tāniko weaving in two, three or four colours.

I am indebted to Mrs Rangimarie Hetet of Te Kuiti for helping me in the 1960s when her hands (see plate 7) were still comparatively youthful, and when it was still possible for a man to study weaving. Today Māori women are quite rightly taking command of the taonga handed down to us through the female line. This book has served a useful purpose in providing some information for the people who were keen to learn at a time when there were no books available. Perhaps the day is not far away when Māori women will produce books that will present tāniko weaving in a more interesting way than I have done here. My task has been to provide a historical background to tāniko.

Numbered cloaks in the text refer to catalogued cloaks in the collection of the Auckland Institute and Museum. At the time the research was done for this book

Mr V.F. Fisher was the ethnologist at Auckland. His help is remembered today and appreciated. I acknowledge also the Ethnographic Museum of Stockholm for plate 25, and the assistance given in the 1960s by a number of people: Mrs Ponga Chadwick, Mrs Joy Biggs, Mrs Dick George, Mrs Anne Whaipooti, Mrs W. Stirling, Mr W. Hohepa, Mrs du Tait, Mr G.A. McCracken, Mr C.A. Schollum and my wife June Te Rina.

Tāniko weaving is a taonga handed down by the ancestors to us of today. As a taonga it will always remain a treasure of great value that will be there waiting to be touched again, warmed and given a new lease of life. It will never tire of us, even though many of us will grow impatient and tired of tāniko. May the rising of the sun to herald a new day give warmth to this taonga.

Hirini Moko Mead

Preface to the 2019 edition

When *Te Whatu Tāniko* was first published my father dedicated the book to me, and that dedication has been retained through the book's many revised editions, which have spanned most of my life.

As a child it felt great to see a book dedicated to me, but I did not feel any responsibility for the contents, and my own attempts at tāniko have been shameful failures. Now the responsibility has been passed to me, casually I might say, by my father telling me, 'It is time. I think you should write this foreword. Here is the book.' And here I am, the child to whom a book was once dedicated, no longer a child but a woman looking at old age.

The book has proven to be relevant through several decades and to resonate with new audiences across the generations. It is worth asking, 'why?'. While my own tāniko skills did not blossom, my interest in Māori cultural regeneration, in mātauranga Māori, and in decolonising and indigenous research methodologies, did become a focus of my career as a scholar.

Over the decades that have been spanned by the different editions of *Te Whatu Tāniko*, Māori culture, te Reo Māori, toi Māori, tā moko tikanga and mātauranga Māori have inspired and informed Māori aspirations for mana motuhake and self-determination. As Māori people, as whānau, hapū and iwi, we have searched for recognition, for justice, and for the tools to develop ourselves. As we have navigated the challenges of the times we have consistently expressed our unique Māori-ness, our identity, through our arts and voice, through the weaving of our past with dreams of the future, through the use of old and new materials and techniques, and the design and use of our patterns, motifs, symbols, and stories.

Against the gamut of what constitutes Māori cultural heritage, tāniko weaving might be seen to be rather insignificant. But it stands alongside tā moko, whakairo rakau, kapa haka and weaving beautiful cloaks as images of our world that we can actually engage with, touch physically, create ourselves and wear when we want to emphasise we are Māori. Tāniko work has its own beauty when woven with pride and exhibiting masterly control of the artform. It is as relevant now as it was when this book was first published.

Readers seem interested not only in the techniques of tāniko, but in the stories of tāniko, the meaning and significance of tāniko, the tikanga of tāniko and the mātauranga of tāniko. These have mostly been nurtured by our women. There are new generations of experts in tāniko, some of whom I am honoured to know as the daughters, granddaughters and great-granddaughters of the women who first instructed my father on their practices of rāranga. Hopefully this edition of *Te Whatu Tāniko* will inspire and instruct another generation, not only to create tāniko but also to wear it as part of our everyday clothing.

Linda Tuhiwai Smith
May 2019

1

An Introduction to Māori Costume

If you attend a Māori concert in some public hall in New Zealand, or the ceremonial complex held in conjunction with the coronation celebrations at Ngaruawahia every October, or the cultural competitions associated with church festivals such as the Anglican Hui Tōpu, or the opening ceremonies of a new carved meeting house, or should you be present when ministerial, vice-regal or royal visitors are being entertained on Māori ground, you will find performers dressed in a manner that immediately marks them as being distinct from the spectators. These teams of dancers welcome or entertain with performances of war dances, action songs, chants and poi dances.[1] The teams consist of men and women, or boys and girls, whose ages may range from five to sixty years. In most cases the performers are Māori, but one should not be surprised to discover Pākehā New Zealanders or Cook Islanders or Fijians in such teams. By and large, however, the performances are a peculiarly Māori occupation and form part of Māori cultural expression. Even concert parties performing for tourists or general audiences do so to raise funds for some community or village project such as building a carved meeting house.

When a team of men and women perform publicly, it is customary for them to adopt Māori costume. The more important the occasion the stronger is the pressure upon them to assume 'proper' costume. While so dressed, the performers regard themselves as wearing a kind of ritual costume; it is not only a matter of entering into the spirit of the occasion, but it is one of historical and cultural significance that they feel intuitively. The costume has roots in the distant past of the Māori, which goes back well beyond the era of Captain Cook (1769).

Women in a performing team (usually referred to colloquially as a Māori culture group) wear headbands, with or without feathers, neck pendants known as the tiki, ear pendants of shark teeth, bodices in tāniko patterns, kilts of flax, and an underskirt in red or black. No footwear, anklets or bracelets are worn. Plate 1 illustrates modern Māori costume for women.

As a maximum outfit, men wear a headband with a feather or feathers, a bandolier patterned in tāniko, a kilt worn over a pair of shorts and perhaps a cloak. Faces may be painted to represent tattoo marks. When men are actually performing, their costume may consist minimally of shorts and kilt only.

A dominant feature of present-day costume is the use of geometrical patterns, traditionally in red, black and white. The patterns occurring today in headbands, belts, bandoliers and women's bodices are called tāniko patterns. Tāniko refers to both technique and result. There was a time when confusion between the two was not possible because tāniko patterns could be produced only by the tāniko technique. Today, however, tāniko patterns can be produced by a variety of techniques — tapestry, painting, lino cutting, silk-screening, applique and commercial printing. It is therefore necessary to make a clear distinction between the form of the patterns and the technique used to achieve such forms.

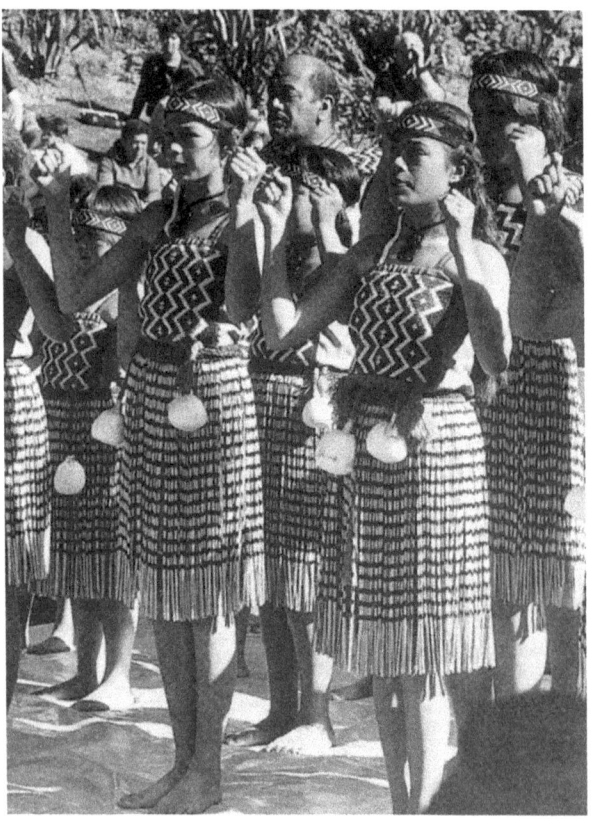

The tāniko technique refers to a specialised method of weaving, by which ornamentation was made possible. Māori did not use looms, so heddles, shuttles and the spinning of weaving material were quite unknown in the culture. However, *Phormium tenax*, a native flax plant, grew in abundant quantities and thus provided the fibres for cloak making and tāniko weaving. Māori weavers evolved a system of finger weaving (also called downward weaving) by which to change the weaving shed for each individual crossing of a weft thread over a warp. With this method, weavers were able to construct very elaborate and often beautiful geometrical patterns. In Māori society, therefore, tāniko weaving was a medium of creative expression for both men and women. It was not as spectacular and as relatively free as wood carving, but it did provide a creative outlet and a means of allowing weavers an opportunity of making a name

Plate 1 The culture team of the Pakipaki Bilingual School, Hawke's Bay, performing at the opening ceremonies for Te Herenga Waka Marae, 6 December 1986.

John Casey

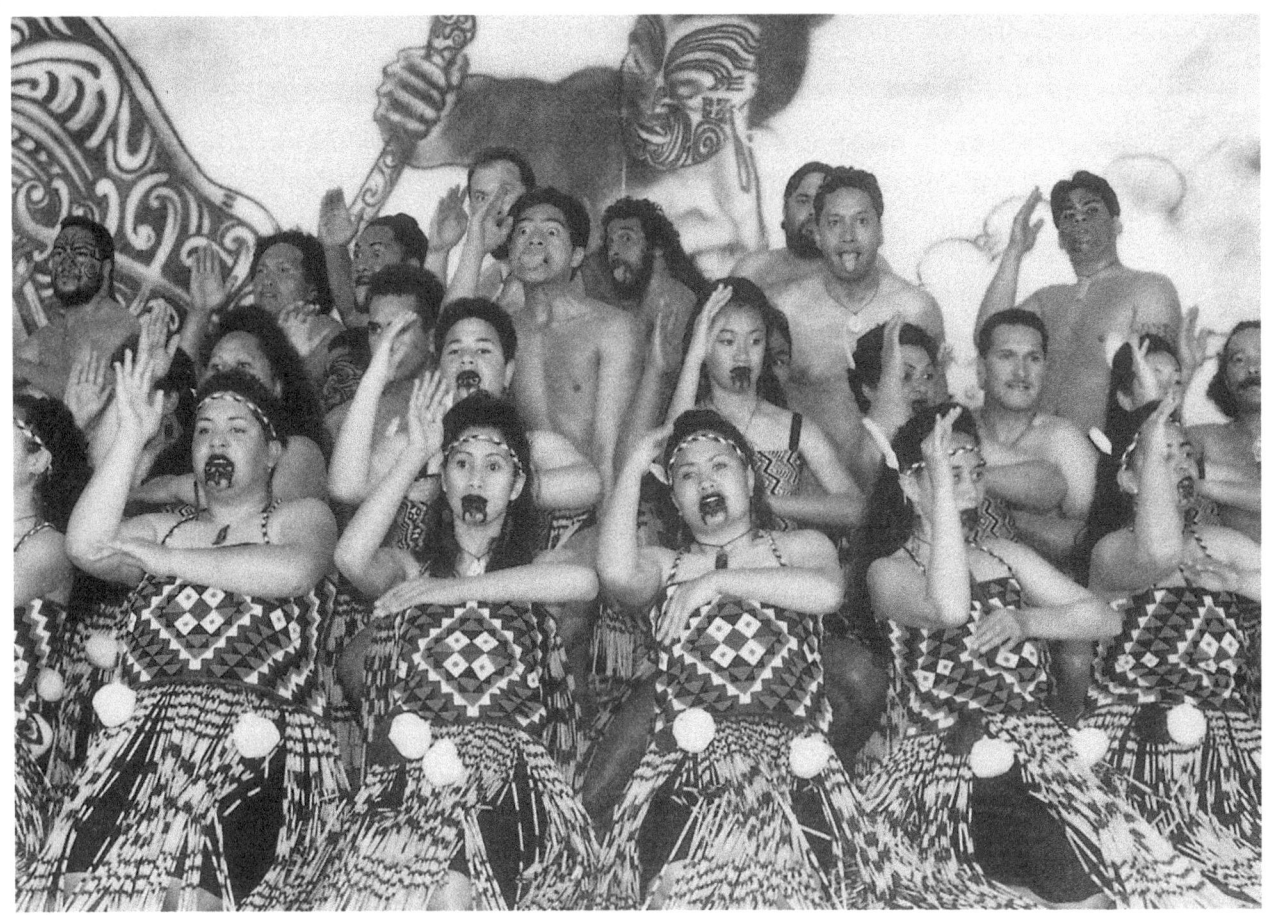

Plate 2 Modern costume of Te Whare Wānanga o Awanuiarangi culture team 1995.
Tapestry weaving was used to make the bodices seen here.
W. Tilley

for themselves. This traditional creative activity continues today but on a much-reduced scale. The era of the general weaver is fast disappearing in New Zealand; specialists are taking over. This is already evident in the manufacture of cloaks and kilts, and to some extent the same thing is happening in tāniko weaving.

However, one suspects that even in the era of general weaving up to the first two decades of the present century there were mediocre, competent and exceptional weavers. This is to be expected in most creative activities. In the 1960s, among the weavers I knew were two exceptional tāniko weavers — Mrs Rangimarie Hetet of Te Kuiti and Mrs Dick George of Waiomatatini who reigned supreme over a 25-year period. Both have passed on but in their day they were technical virtuosos. Boas rightly reminds us that '... artistic work begins after the technical problem has been mastered'.[2] Both of the two exponents of tāniko mentioned above had complete mastery over technique and both were able to play with form and technique in such a way as to produce articles that were eyed covetously by other Māori women. Many new weavers have taken their places.

In following sections of the book the technique of tāniko is described and discussed, and in chapter eight instructions are provided for learning it. Methods formerly employed in preparing fibres and in dyeing them preparatory to weaving are described in some detail. I have followed up the somewhat speculative matter of how the tāniko weave evolved because other scholars have made this a particular issue. Much less speculative is the survey of the history and development of tāniko up to the present time. This section draws attention to the fact that as people change the objects they use tend to change too. People and their cultures do not remain static. The generation of Māori performers who use Māori costume will be able to appreciate that the costume articles they use now and label as traditional are really vastly changed from their Classical period counterparts, and are often, as in the case of the bodice and bandolier, entirely fresh innovations, with no counterpart in Classical times. This leads to the realisation suspected by few that tradition is often very shallow in terms of time. It appears that in Māori society an event is classified as traditional if our grandparents or parents were witnesses of it and partakers in it. There is nothing wrong with this attitude, however. The error has been in not understanding how tradition operates in Māori society; in why, how and which events become traditionalised.

Other scholars interested in tāniko, such as Buck, Phillipps and Barrow, have had something to say about the classification of tāniko patterns according to dominant motif. The pioneer work was done by Buck in 1911 and others have added to it and modernised it in the light of further evidence. Basically, this is what I do in chapter six.

The naming of patterns has always been an area where rival weavers accuse one tribe of stealing the other's patterns. Generally, the motifs used in tāniko patterns are the common property of all tribes and, furthermore, these are arranged in characteristic ways that serve to mark the distinctiveness of Māori work from that of any other ethnic group, say of the Indonesians. But it must be conceded that certain motif arrangements including minute points of detail may be the favourites of a particular locality. Ngāti Porou tribe, for example, lay strong claim to the papaki-rango pattern (pattern 13 in chapter six) as being traditionally their property. The claim is probably a just one because weavers in this area do seem to have their own interpretation of this common arrangement. In many cases, however, the disputed pattern arrangements have a wide distribution under many different labels. Weavers of a particular stylistic area were able to discuss patterns by names that were unintelligible to outside weavers and so, by a device of language, they could act as though the patterns were tribal property.

The instructional section in chapter eight is, in a sense, a test of how well I know the technique of tāniko weaving. The plan adopted here is to describe the making of a sampler that takes in all the essential techniques that occur in the process. It is assumed that, having successfully manufactured the sampler, the student is able to apply the same body of techniques to the making of other articles. Extra techniques have been provided so that an area of choice is available to those students who want to fulfil the Boas requirement of mastery over technique.

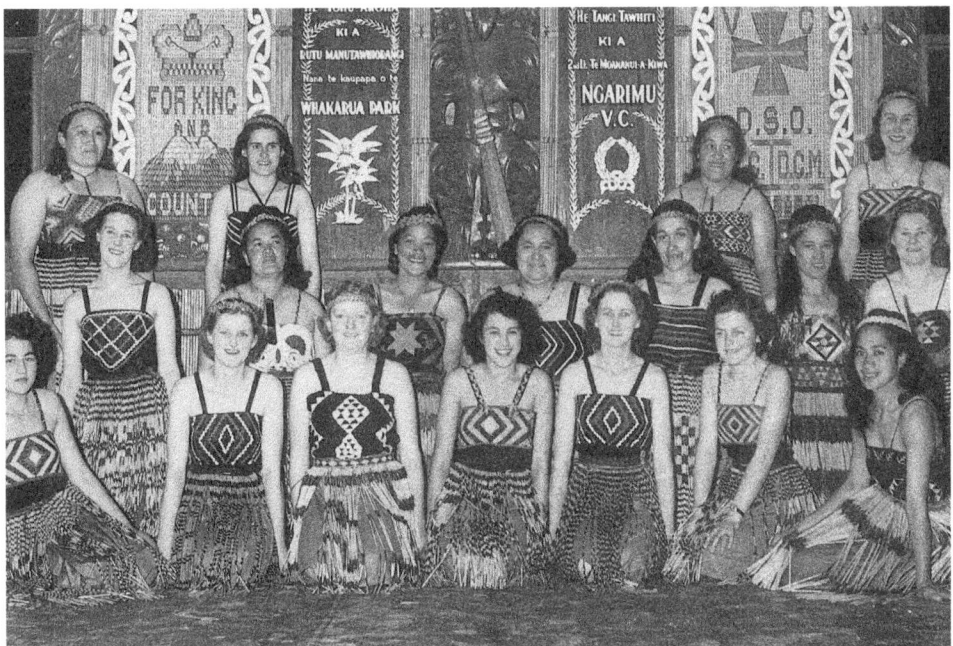

Plate 3 Costume for performing teams in 1947. This is a group from Ruatoria after the opening of Uepohatu in 1947. Tapestry weaving was already in wide use at the time among Ngāti Porou teams. E mihi ana ki te hunga kua wehe ki te po.
Weekly News

The components of Māori costume

Modern Māori costume consists of garments, hanging ornaments, feathers and applied decorations such as painted tattoo. The most essential item of costume in both male and female attire is the kilt or piupiu.

Essentially, the piupiu is made of cylindrical strands of dried flax, each one scraped and dyed at intervals and the whole forming an overall pattern. The suspended strands are attached to a waistband, which holds them securely in place. Piupiu for men are above the knee in length (plate 4) and either knee length or just below for women.

While still green, each strand is scraped at intervals spaced according to a predetermined pattern, which is often laid out on a piece of flat board. When put out to dry the unscraped portions curl over to form stiff tubes. The scraped portions provide 'give' in each strand. After the strands are assembled and attached to a waistband the whole garment is left for some days to dry out slowly. The dried-out kilt is then dipped into a hot mordant of whīnau bark for some hours and then into black mud containing iron. The scraped fibres turn black and the unscraped portions remain a golden colour, thus producing patterns of gold and black (plate 1). The colouring depends very much on the quality of flax used.

Piupiu strands are nowadays always patterned in some way or other, usually in a bold pattern that can be seen clearly from a distance. It has not always been like this. The waistband may be decorated with tāniko, but in the majority of cases it is not. There are two qualities of kilts that are important in ceremonies: the display of geometric designs; and the rustling noise the strands make as the dancer moves to and fro. Associated with the first is a certain amount of symbolism, the patterns serving to mark the wearer as a Māori, and in some cases also marking what group the dancer belongs to.

In female costume, the bodice is now of almost equal importance. It consists usually of a rectangular piece of tapestry cloth that forms the foundation for tāniko patterns themselves and structurally for the garment as well. It is lined with soft material, shoulder-straps are attached, and hooks and eyes are sewn to the back to secure the bodice in place. The lining material is allowed to hang below the bodice so that it can be tucked into the piupiu, thus covering the stomach completely.

This part of the costume is relatively new, having been adopted only after the Māori population became Christianised. Not until this century did the bodice become a standardised piece of costume. It has gone through several evolutionary changes. Early attempts made in the cloak-making technique were at first modelled on the blouses of pioneer women and proved very awkward garments. Later, brassieres were used as the

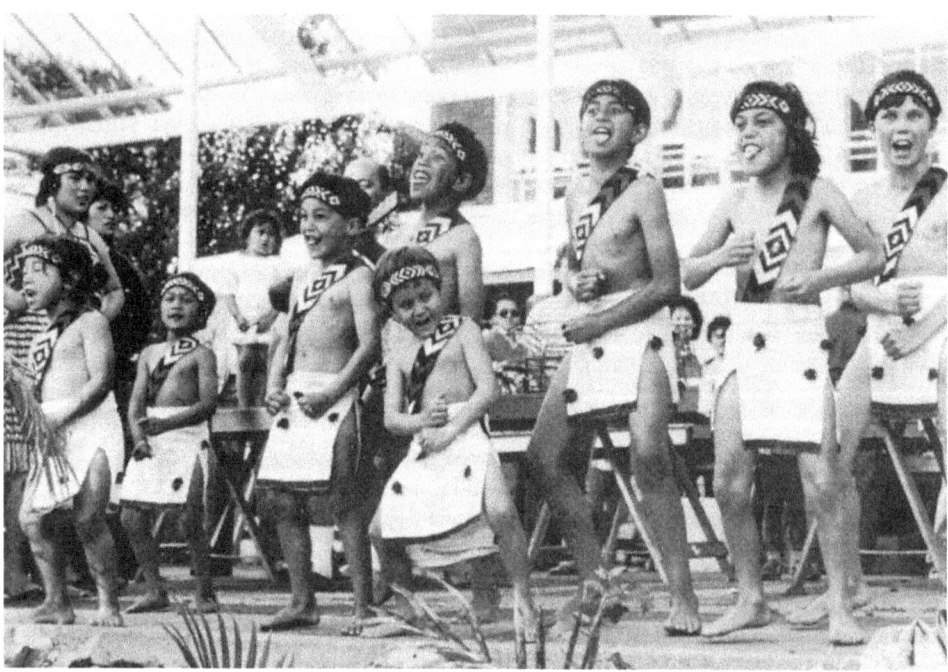

Plate 4 Boys of Pakipaki Bilingual School display the costume that is popular today for male performers. The occasion is the opening of Te Herenga Waka Marae, Victoria University.
John Casey

model. Techniques of manufacture have, in the main, ranged from the cloak-making technique employing feathers as decoration to the tāniko technique proper to produce tāniko patterns in red, black and white, and, later, to the tapestry weave. The tapestry method of producing tāniko patterns on bodices is illustrated in plates 1–3.

Headbands are worn by both men and women. Formerly, two kinds were used: the ornate, made with the tāniko technique, and the simple, made from green flax blades and sometimes preferred for male costume. The ornate headband is now usually made with tapestry (plate 1). Feathers may be worn with the headband by both men and women. Feathers in the hair have a long association with Māori costume, going back to at least 1642, when Dutchman Abel Tasman came to New Zealand.

Suspended ornaments are mainly represented by the neck pendant known as the tiki. In Classical Māori times this ornament was made of whalebone or greenstone. Genuinely old tiki have a very high heirloom value, and women who own them are greatly envied by the have-nots. Tiki have been used continuously as neck ornaments for some 200 years and form one of the oldest elements of present-day Māori costume.

Here again, however, the fact of change cannot be avoided. The demand for tiki pendants by an increasing number of Māori culture teams is being met commercially. Plastic tiki were used in the 1960s but are now replaced with commercially produced greenstone tiki.

In some teams the women wear shark-teeth pendants from which hang long black ribbons. Shark-teeth pendants have an association with the Māori quite as long as the tiki, and they too help to give historical significance to the costume.

When Captain Cook came upon them in 1769, men and women who had full citizen rights were tattooed in deep indelible lines of green-black or blue-black. By custom, women's tattoo were confined to the lips and chin, but men were permitted full facial and buttock tattoo if they had earned the right to it. Tattooing was strongly condemned by the missionaries and so the early decades of the twentieth century witnessed the disappearance of elaborate male tattoo. Concert parties, however, still perpetuate the custom. Women paint their lips and chin with blue or black eyebrow pencil, and men paint their faces with black eyebrow pencil in the appropriate designs. With the resurgence in ta moko (tattooing) many performers are now ornamented with permanent moko.

Cloaks are sometimes worn as a maximal item. The genuine product is, however, difficult to acquire and there are few performers who could afford to purchase such articles; so a compromise is necessary. Groups make their own very cheaply by using commercially made materials.

Another item of present-day Māori costume without a counterpart in the Classical Māori period is the bandolier, an item of male costume modelled on bandoliers worn by British troops. It is now made with the tapestry technique and features tāniko patterns. An example may be seen in plate 4.

Headbands, bodices and bandoliers feature tāniko patterns. Some 30 years ago kilt waistbands were also decorated with tāniko. These are the items with which this study is mainly concerned, but cloaks can not be ignored because they have been the main field of tāniko application since pre-contact days.

In age and historical significance, tāniko patterns rank with white gannet feathers in the hair, indelible facial tattoo, and with ornaments such as the tiki and shark-teeth ear pendants. Such patterns were being produced as cloak decorations at the time Cook rediscovered New Zealand in 1769 but, like other sections of Māori costume, these patterns have undergone changes in technique, material and in motifs. These will become apparent in the discussion in chapter four.

By describing the whole costume we have placed tāniko into the cultural complex that gives it most meaning. The geometrical patterns in red, black and white are a necessary part of costume expression. As a distinctive marker of Māori costume they are particularly conspicuous. They are valued because of long association with the past of the people. Tāniko woven objects, however, are not connected only with dancing. Other articles, such as belts, serviette rings, purses and pulpit decorations in churches, are also made. The craft is taught in many schools and is fostered by many women's organisations.

Notes
1. In these dances female performers twirl balls suspended with string. There are several varieties of poi dances — single, double, long or short.
2. Boas, 1955, p. 65.

2

The Tāniko
Weaving Technique

A detailed step-by-step description of the tāniko technique as practised in modern times is provided in chapter eight. Remarks here, therefore, will be aimed at giving a general description in terms of the past.

When the weaver holds a piece of work during manufacture, the warp threads (whenu) hang downward, and the weft (aho) run transversely from left to right. The warps are arranged along the first weft row, called aho tapu (sacred weft), by a technique of interlocking with a two-pair weft. Each warp element is secured during this casting-on stage at two places; first, near the middle after which the top end is folded down, and again near the fold. Figure 3 on page 31 illustrates the technique. When the desired length is reached and the last fold is secured, the foundation weft is tied. For smaller work, this was all that was generally required for setting-up the work.

For larger work it was advisable to free the hands of the worker completely so that she could concentrate on weaving. To expedite this the traditional method was to stretch the work across two weaving pegs (turuturu), which were stuck into the ground or leaned against a wall.

For still larger work a further refinement was necessary to avoid stretching the line of warps. The problem was solved by stretching a single thread, called aho tāhuhu, across the weaving pegs before the warps were cast on. This thread was then incorporated into the casting-on stage by folding the warp elements over it, so that the completed line of warps was suspended by their folds and not by the first weft.

The preparation of each row of weft elements depended on the number of colours in the design to be worked. A two-colour pattern required a weft having two colours and a three-colour pattern required a weft of three colours. In addition an extra passive thread may be added to each weft line. The passive thread runs along behind the warp threads and is used for tightening the weft row as required and especially at the conclusion of the row. The active threads are twisted around each warp element in accordance with the principle that one rotation of the wrist when a two-colour weft is being worked changes the colour, and two rotations brings forward the same colour. No matter how many elements make up each weft row there can be only one of these showing on the front of the warp, and that one is the colour-carrying element. The others are kept out of sight behind the warp. Technically speaking, a piece of tāniko work consists of hundreds of half and full twists around the warps. Generally, since the left hand of the weaver holds the warp in position and the right hand manipulates the weft elements of each row, this process can be translated in terms of action as a series of single and double rotations of the right hand and wrist.

The characteristic twisting of the wrist and threads prompted the author to describe the process as tāniko 'twisting'. Ling Roth, author of *The Maori Mantle* (1923), preferred the term 'twining', which he thought much more appropriate than 'weaving'. Following

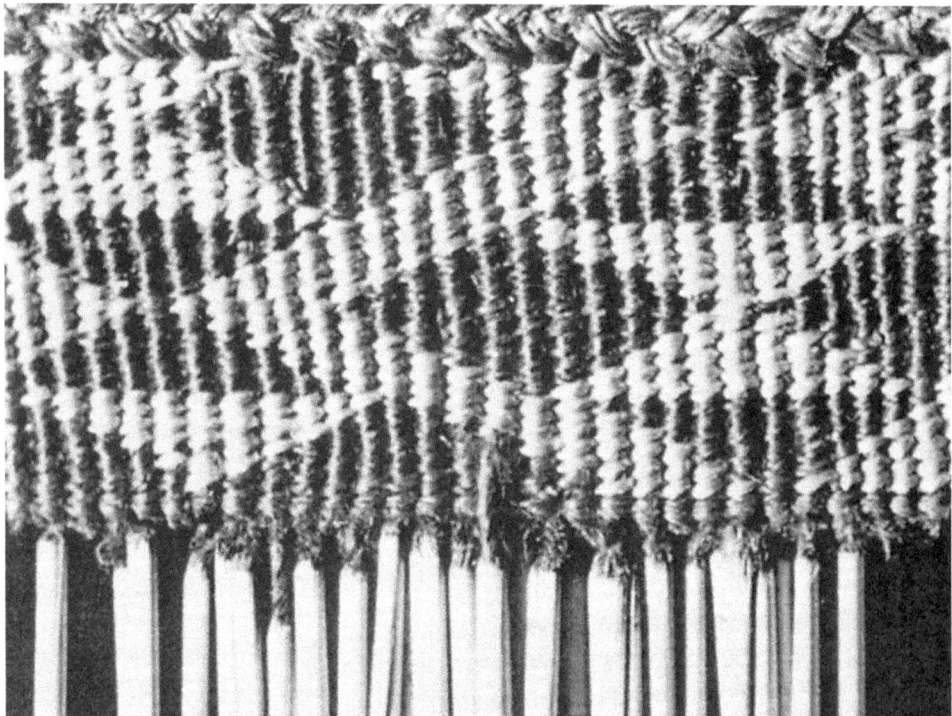

Plate 5 Tāniko band of a kilt, probably made in the late Transitional period, or very early in the Modern period, by a Ngāti Maniapoto weaver. The strands are old and tattered, but the pattern made in dyed flax fibre stands out clearly. The garment belongs to the personal collection of Mrs Joy Biggs of Ngāti Maniapoto. The top ends of the flax strands form the vertical warps of the tāniko pattern.
C.A. Schollum

Roth, Buck used the term 'wrapped twine' in much of his writing on tāniko weaving. As already mentioned, the terms 'finger weaving' and 'downward weaving' have also been applied to the technique. The descriptive terms invented so far appear to suffer some deficiency or other; for example, twisting or twining does not cover all weaving actions in tāniko work. The two-pair interlocking weft stroke, a standard technique in tāniko, is neither twine nor twist. Moreover, tāniko weaving may be done from the bottom upwards or on a horizontal plane, so that 'downward weaving' is not satisfactory either. I propose to call the technique simply tāniko weaving. The justification for adhering to the use of 'weaving' is that the two-pair interlocking stroke is true weaving involving the changing of 'sheds' but the mechanics employed by Māori weavers are simple. No useful purpose is to be gained by coining a new label for tāniko weaving.

An examination of plate 5 will give some idea of the result of tāniko weaving. The photograph shows in detail a tāniko band of a kilt made either very late in the nineteenth century or early in the twentieth. Running vertically are the warps, the tops of which are just visible at the top of the photograph. Follow any one warp line down to the bottom and you will notice how it has been covered over, line by line, by wefts of different colours. In this case two colours have been used, so that there would always be at least one, and possibly two, weft threads running behind the warps, and one in front. If four colours were used there would be three threads behind and one in front, and so on. The wefts run horizontally. Taking any one weft line and proceeding from left to right, you will notice that the threads have been woven around every warp thread encountered.

The tāniko weave produces a stiff fabric, which was considered unsuitable by the Māori of old for wearing next to the skin. Consequently, its use was confined to the borders of cloaks as a purely decorative element. The fact that every warp thread had to be crossed by a weft explains to a great extent why tāniko patterns tend to be rectilinear as opposed to the curvilinear patterns used in tattoo and wood carving. Using the tāniko weave it was comparatively easy to form triangles, oblique lines, diamonds, rectangles and straight lines, but it was not so easy to reproduce the curves of a rafter pattern, though this is done now in modern work. The patterns produced in tāniko work are very similar to the patterns used in basketry and decorative reed work (tukutuku).

So far we have learnt that tāniko is a simple form of weaving. The fabric produced by this technique is stiff and unsuitable for wearing next to the skin, hence its use as decorative borders of superior cloaks like the kaitaka and paepaeroa. Because wefts (aho) cross warp (whenu) threads, the patterns produced tend to be based on straight-line arrangements. Several colours may be used. A composite weft line may carry three colours or more or less. The only aids used are the weaving sticks, turuturu, and passive threads carried behind each weft line, which are pulled to tighten and strengthen the work.

Materials used

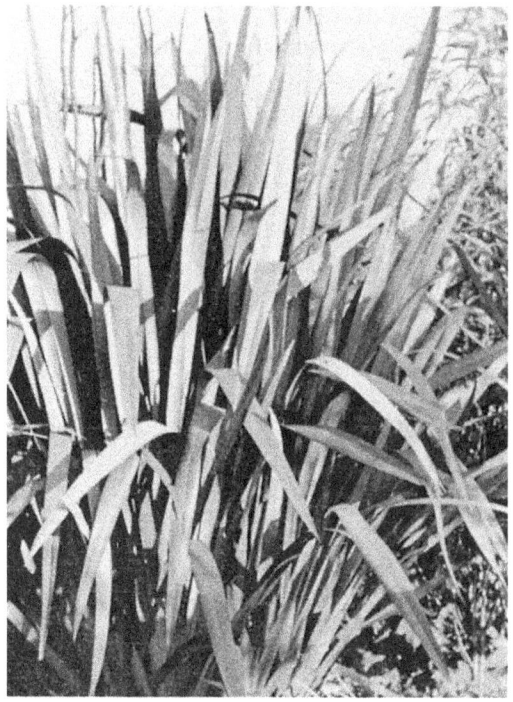

Plate 6 A stand of Phormium tenax of the variety known as kōhunga, which provides excellent fibre for high-quality weaving.

C.A. Schollum

When Captain Cook first saw the Māori they were still using tapa cloth but not as a clothing material. The few pieces noted by Cook and botanist Joseph Banks were being used as highly valued ear ornaments. For clothing, the material in general use then was flax, known among Māori as harakeke. A highly exploited plant, the flax (*Phormium tenax*) provided the friable material for the manufacture of kilts, cloaks, belts, kits, floor mats and nets of various sizes. Its rhizome was used as a medicine to combat constipation; the sticky gum at the base of the leaves was used to cover burns; the stalks were utilised as floats or as torches; and the leaves, besides having those uses already listed, was a general lashing material. The fact that the paper mulberry tree failed to flourish in New Zealand led to an easy adoption of flax as a substitute.

Many varieties were known. The Flax Commission's Report of 1871[1] listed 47 named varieties.Varieties suitable for tāniko weaving were those which were used for the manufacture of superior garments. A variety known as atirau kawa and recognised on the East Coast, Taranaki and Opunake had a high-quality fibre. The young leaf is a bright olive-green while the mature leaf turned a bronzy colour, sometimes relieved by a bright red line. The oue variety known to weavers in Taranaki, Hawke's Bay, Waikato and the East Coast had a narrow leaf, olive-green in colour, with the edge and keel fading on the upper side. It was similar to a variety known as kōhunga in the Waikato-Maniapoto area (plate 6) and tīhore in the Raglan and Taranaki districts.[2] Tregear listed as the best varieties for high-quality garments the tihoi, oue, rongo-tainui, rukutia and huruhika,[3] but unfortunately, no identification marks were given. Tihoi, however, would appear to be the same as tīhore and Tregear's oue variety is probably the same as that identified by the Flax Commission.

The first step in the preparation of weaving elements is to cut from a superior variety, such as the oue, unmarked leaves from one year to 18 months old. The outer decay in leaves of the plant known as pakawhā were cut and discarded to allow other leaves a chance to grow freely. For obvious reasons the very young leaves, called rito, which grew in the centre of the plant were quite unsuitable for weaving. When a bundle of muka (fibre) leaves had been collected it was carried home by the weaver. Near the safety and comfort of her home she would begin the slow task of stripping each blade and extracting the white fibre. From each complete leaf the edges and midrib were removed and the fibre was extracted by one of two methods, or a combination of both.

1. The hāro method

A light cut is made across the underside of a strand of flax about halfway along its length. The flax strand is held securely by the left hand immediately behind the cut (plate 7A). A mussel shell held in the right hand is placed over the top surface of the flax strand opposite the cut as shown in plate 7A. Then slowly the shell is dragged over the blade in an outward motion, for about 12–13 centimetres. This action causes the underside to separate. To facilitate the easy removal of the fibre from this point, a loop is made in the underpart, as shown in the photograph, and then with one final sweep of the right hand the waste material from the blade is stripped off. Plate 7C illustrates the result. The waste underside can be seen in the photograph. After this, the blade of flax is turned around and the process is repeated on the other half. The removed portion

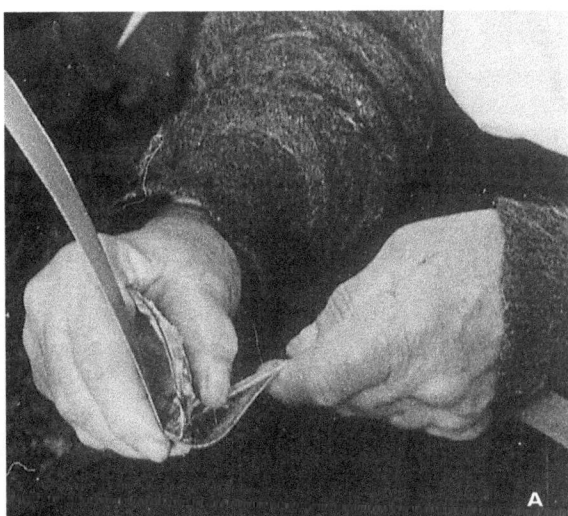

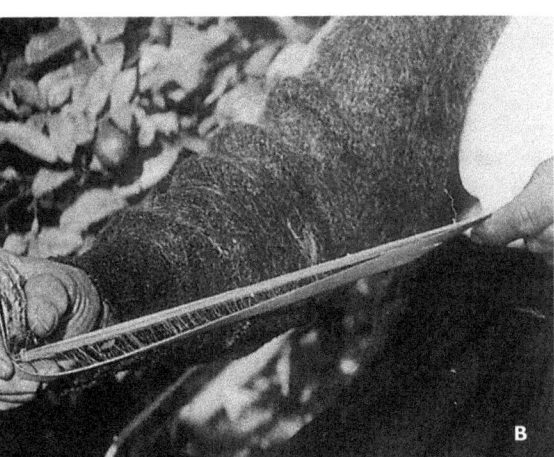

Plates 7A, 7B, 7C Mrs Hetet of Te Kuiti demonstrates the hāro method. Here she shows the beginning of the process and the end of the first sweep.
C.A. Schollum

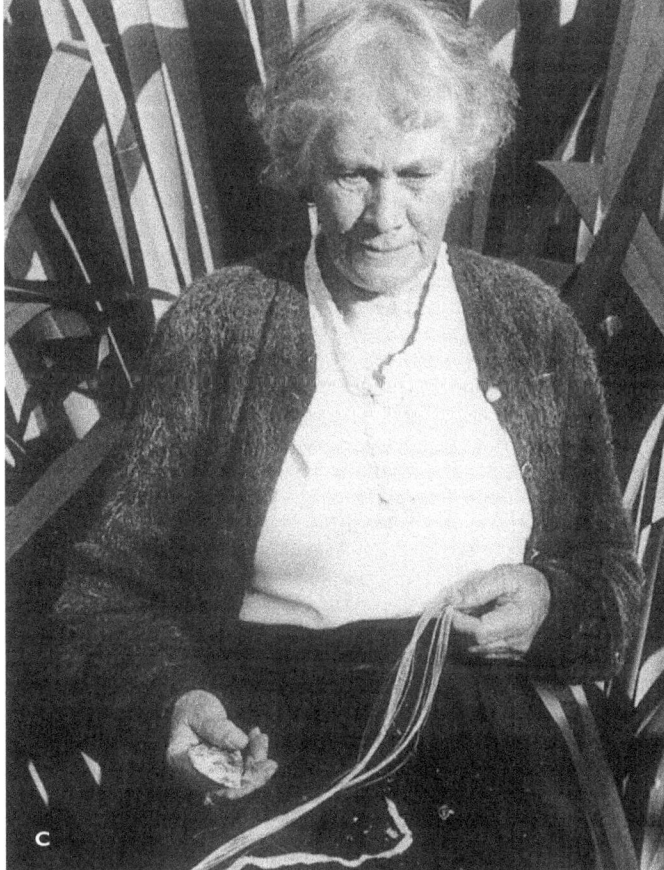

(that is, the green cuticle) was formerly used as tags for rain cloaks. With light scraping, these sections turned a golden colour when dry.

If the hāro method was skilfully performed, little further scraping was necessary to clean the fibres completely.

When a sufficient quantity of fibres was so prepared they were given a final scraping and a thorough washing. Beating with a wooden or stone pounder upon a rounded well-worn river stone followed.[4]

2. The takiri method

The takiri method of removing fibre is used most successfully only with certain kinds of flax. A cut is made on the underside, as before, and then the flax blade is folded over so that the cut opens out. While the folded piece is held in the left hand the top half is grasped in the right hand. The top half is pressed firmly down against the left hand, while at the same time it is drawn away from the area of the cut. This action causes the lower portion of the flax to separate from the upper. When the weaver sees that the separation has begun smoothly, her two hands jerk suddenly away from each other, continuing the action until separation is complete. The process is repeated for the other half. This jerking movement is called takiri. As with the hāro method, the fibres are thoroughly scraped afterwards, but the advantage of takiri method is that the scraping is reduced to a minimum.

After being thoroughly scraped the fibre is washed, and then scraped again to make the fibres absolutely clean and white. Then they are dried, whakamaroke, and separated into hanks, whakaio, which are convenient for storage or as working lots. They are now ready for use, and many cloaks were manufactured of fibre prepared only to this stage. However, if a softer fibre is required, then they are washed again.

The treatment is followed by a period of beating with stone pounders on flat water-worn river stones. The pounders are called either patu muka or patu whitau. Then the fibres are washed, dried and hanked. The raw material for all white wefts is then ready for use.

Tregear makes a distinction between the two words for prepared fibre, muka and whitau; the latter, he maintains, is fully prepared fibre and the former is a general word for flax fibre. However, Williams's *A Dictionary of the Maori Language* makes no such distinction, except to add that whitau was used especially in reference to the fibres of the variety called takikau or tīhore,[5] which can be stripped by the takiri method. This addition suggests that Tregear was probably correct in making the distinction.

Rolling the fibre into cords

Although much has been written by Best and Hamilton on the Māori method of preparing weaving threads, the information is usually lacking in some essential details. The Māori method, in its general feature, is not unique; other primitive societies, namely some in New Guinea and New Britain, employ a similar technique.

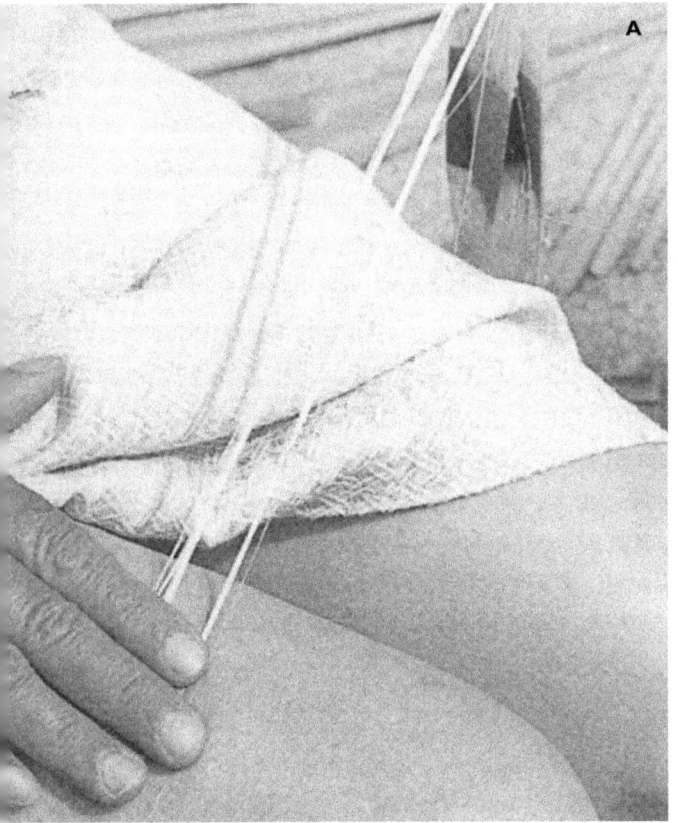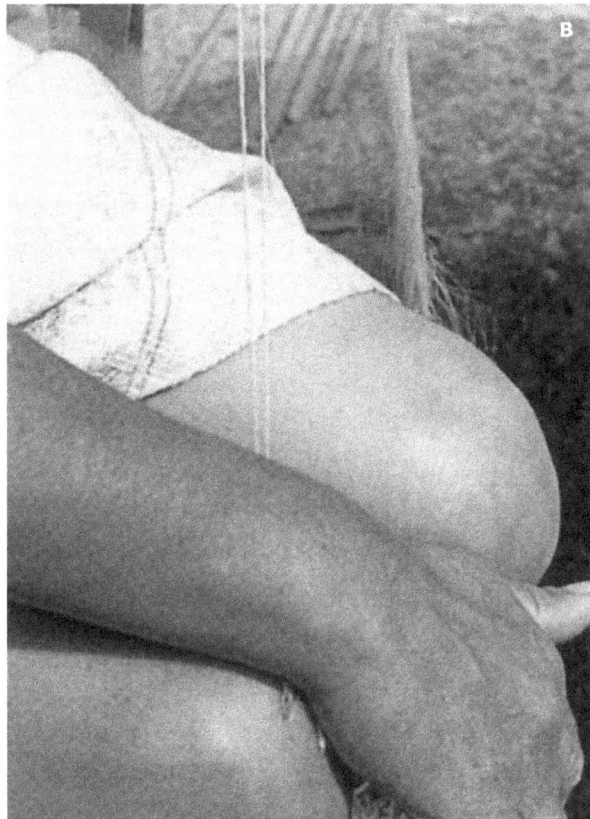

Plates 8A, 8B The first part of the rolling process. The action here is the katau, that is, forward from the body, down the leg and to the right of the leg. The forward action is almost complete.

C.A. Schollum

However, there are some points of detail that are probably peculiar to the Māori.

The thickness of the cords depends on how many individual fibres are rolled together, so it is important to work this out beforehand. For warp threads a usual number is 18 to 20, and for weft threads about 10. As individual fibres taper towards the top end it is essential to top and tail them in order to produce threads of even thickness.

The total number of individual fibres are halved, two lots of five for weft and two lots of nine for the thicker warp threads. These halved sections have one end held in the left hand while the other end is placed over the right leg just above the knee. The two sections are 5 centimetres apart. Then the fingers of the free right hand are placed over the fibres and pressure is applied against the skin of the thigh. Pushing gently against the skin and at the same time using the left hand to keep some tension on the two lots of fibre, the weaver now pushes her hand forward away from her body. As she does so, the fibres begin to roll under her fingers then under the palm of the hand and finally past the wrist and along the arm. By this time the fibres are down the leg below the knee.

The return movement from below the knee to the starting position now fuses the two halves into a thread consisting of two parts (plates 5A and B). Such a thread is called miro, which Māori weavers insist is a single thread, and so ethnographers have erroneously classed miro as a single-ply thread. The point to keep in mind is that a miro thread is one produced by the method just outlined.

A double miro thread, known as karure,[6] is produced by rolling two miro threads together. Miro is produced in the order of forward and rightward action followed by backward and leftward action; in Māori terminology, katau (right) plus mauī (left). To produce karure threads the order of rolling is reversed to mauī followed by katau. This time the fusing action is the final outward or tatau movement.

Extra lengths are added to the thread by simply rolling them in with the appropriate series of rolling movements depending on whether miro or karure are wanted.

According to Buck,[7] it is usual for the warp threads of rain, tag and feather cloaks to be rolled with a loose two-ply twist. Then these cords are beaten again, and then rubbed between the hands (kōmiri) until they become very crinkly. The important thing for the experimenter to know is that when each warp will no longer straighten out, that is, when it remains crinkly, it is ready for use in any of the above cloaks. Generally speaking, the border was not meant to be in close contact with the skin, so it was not necessary for its warps to be crinkly. Furthermore, such softness would tend to disappear anyway once composite wefts had been attached, so it was rather pointless. The looseness or tension of a two-ply twist is controlled by the application of pressure by the right palm against the thigh during the second movement. The softer the pressure the looser the tension.

Formerly the great bulk of threads used in the manufacture of cloaks would be natural undyed whitau, which is rolled into cords as described above. In relation to a whole cloak very little dyed material was needed. However, if a tāniko border was required, then some of the cords or the fibres would have to be dyed as colour contrasts were used to produce patterns.

How the fibres were dyed

The patterns of tāniko borders in cloaks such as the kaitaka and paepaeroa were worked by varying the colours brought forward to cover each warp. In very old work there was more black used than any other colour, and even now black remains the dominant colour, although there is less of it used. Various colours were used in conjunction with black; some yellow, red, and some natural fibre representing white.

We shall deal with the methods used by the Māori for producing these colours. Part of the information supplied here has been gained from informants through questioning and discussions, and part from the works of Best and Buck.

The yellow dye

A yellow dye was obtained from the coprosma tree, usually the karamu. My informants claimed that a richer yellow was obtained from the kanono tree (*Coprosma australis*), which in the pioneer days provided the 'bushmen's iodine'. The roots of the kanono were cut up into small pieces and then cooked in the pungarehu (ashes). When the roots were cooked they became soft, and the juice could be extracted easily from these pieces. It was this juice that was used as a dye, or in lieu of iodine for treating any open wounds or cuts. My informants recalled using kanono juice for tanning leather. For this purpose it was more effective than tānekaha (*Phyllocladus*), but my informants were a little confused over whether the resulting colour was more yellow than red or vice versa.

Both Buck and Tregear mention the coprosma as providing a dye for yellow. Buck says that the bark of the coprosma was used, but he did not specify which coprosma, nor how the bark was used.[8] Tregear says that both the karamu and the raurēkau coprosmas were used and he too mentions that the bark was used.[9] Perhaps it could be assumed that the bark was treated in a similar way to the preparation of tānekaha, described below.

The red dye

According to my informants, a red-brown, described as being a little redder than the colour of varnish, was obtained by soaking the fibres in an infusion of tānekaha. Apparently Māori farmers of the East Coast used to tan their animal hides in this same mixture leaving each hide in the dye bath for two nights before drying. Best describes how the mixture was prepared[10]: the bark was pounded and then boiled in a wooden bowl (kumete). Heated stones were placed in the bowl and when the mixture boiled the prepared fibres were put into it and left there to soak. The fibres were then taken out of the mixture and rolled in hot clean ashes or powdered charcoal, after which they were soaked in the tānekaha mixture again.

We are told by Barrow that a deeper colour resulted from the use of the burnt and powdered bark of the taotoa (*Phyllocladus tricomanoides*) but it is not explained how the powdered bark was used. He adds that a golden-brown was obtained by using the bark of a large-leaved karamu-rau-nui (*Coprosma robusta*) instead of tānekaha, in which case rolling in ashes to fix the colour was not necessary.[11]

The black dye

Obtaining a suitable and fast black was a much more complex process than those described so far, and it appears to be the only one which involved some prohibitions on the part of the weaver. A mordant (waitumu) of either makomako (*Aristotelia serrata*), whīnau (*Elaeocarpus dentatus*) or tutu (*Coriaria arborea*) was prepared by pounding the bark upon a flat stone. This crushed bark was mixed with cold water in a wooden bowl. The whitau was immersed in this mixture and left to soak for 12 hours, after which it was hung up to dry.[12] My informant maintained that if the makomako mordant was used, the flax was best left to soak for two nights.

After the flax is soaked in one of the mordants mentioned it is then taken to be dipped into a special black mud. The mud, known as maramara to Buck and as uku to my informants, is rusty coloured on top and is usually to be found in swamps. Some weavers pour a portion of the mordant into the mud and this is then stirred, but this action is really unnecessary. The rust now disappears and the mud changes to a deep black colour and after thorough agitation is ready to be used as a dye. The flax fibre, which has been first treated in the mordant so that it will take a permanent colour, is now dipped into the mud and the strands are manipulated with the hands to ensure that all parts are in contact with it. As each bundle was so handled, it was left in the mud while other bundles were dipped in. Much care and patience was needed for this work.

My informants went on to say that when a patch of mud is used for dyeing purposes for the first time it is usual to immerse the first lot of flax for two nights. Thereafter, one night is sufficient. Buck gave eight to ten hours as the required time.[13] My informants claimed that the dyeing qualities of the mud improve with use – this, however, seems to be true only if the mud is not removed from its site. In Rotorua the mud is transported to the home of the weaver and is stored in old bathtubs; it can be used to dye about 60 kilts, after which it needs to be renewed. After the flax is pulled out of the mud it is washed thoroughly in running water and then dried out in the shade. If the correct procedures have been followed, the flax fibres should be a deep and permanent black.

In the olden days, but apparently not now, the weavers would try to avoid dyeing any fibres in the mud if a southerly wind (te hautonga) was blowing. If by chance this wind blew after the flax was already dipped into the mud, the flax would then be left there until the wind changed. There are two puzzling features about this custom: one, the reason for it, and two, the fact that Buck should have missed it, especially in view of the fact that much of the field work for his articles on netting and basketry was done in the same area where this custom was known. Referring back to the first point: I was unable to discover any origins for the prohibition, except the common-sense one that, as the south wind brought bad weather anyway, it was unwise to commence any outside work. The south wind and the east wind (marangai) were regarded as bad weather quarters in the territory of my informants.

Formerly, too, a prohibition was placed upon married women who handled the mud. They were required to sleep apart from their husbands from the evening before dyeing operations were commenced until the last of the flax was taken out of the mud. It was usual, therefore, for a spinster or for widows to undertake this kind of work on behalf of their married relatives.

The whole operation of dyeing in the black mud apparently caused sufficient anxiety to make rules and prohibitions necessary. The gods must not be offended or the black obtained would not be permanent, and as a consequence the mana of the weaver would diminish and she would be talked about. To be talked about was unbearable. This would be sufficient cause for a woman to lacerate herself and perform the ceremonial tangi, or in retaliation to compose and perform a derisive chant (pātere) against her detractors. In the minds of the weavers there was probably a magical element as well as a chemical substance in the mud which produced the permanent colour, and it followed that extreme care was necessary to make certain the magic worked. It so happened that the procedures they followed were chemically sound.

Notes

1. Leading members of the Commission were T. Kelly and Colonel Haultain, who gathered much ethnographic information. The report was published in *AJHR*, Vol. 11, G-No. 4, 1871.
2. I am grateful to Mrs Rangimarie Hetet of Te Kuiti for this identification.
3. Tregear, 1926, p. 222.
4. The earliest description of flax prepared by this method is by Lieutenant-Governor Philip King in his journal of 1793.
5. Williams, 1957, p. 516.
6. Best, in 1941, p. 516, describes this as a two-ply cord. This is partly true; if the miro thread is regarded as one ply his description would be correct, but a miro consists of two lots of thread twisted together.
7. Buck, 1926, p. 63.
8. Buck, 1926, p. 60.
9. Tregear, 1926, p. 222.
10. Best, 1941, p. 517.
11. Barrow, 1962, in his article 'Taniko Weaving of the New Zealand Maori' in Palette, No. 9, Spring.
12. Buck, 1923, p. 711.
13. Buck, 1923, p. 712.

3

The Discovery of the Tāniko Technique

Buck believed that tāniko weaving developed from the making of dogskin cloaks. He could well have been correct, but there are other possibilities which deserve some attention.

There are any number of old Māori cloaks in the collections of many museums that attest to the fact that cloak manufacture and tāniko weaving went hand in hand. Tāniko was a decorative technique applied to dogskin and kaitaka cloaks. Usually, the tāniko border was an extension of the warp elements of the cloaks and thus formed an integral part of the garment. That there should be close parallels between the techniques of cloak manufacture and tāniko should occasion no surprise.

Commencement methods are essentially the same. Figure 1, for example, illustrates a simple thrum commencement technique used for soft inner garments. Here the warps are attached one by one with the two-pair interlocking weft. Figure 2 illustrates a standard cloak-commencing technique used in most types of cloaks. In this technique, the tops of the warp elements are folded over and secured with the two rows of the two-pair interlocking weft. The tāniko commencement method (figure 3) is a natural development from the selvedge technique (figure 2). Because cloaks required very long warp threads it was not practical to fold each warp in half, nor was there anything to be gained by doing this. Tāniko borders, on the other hand, were usually about 15 centimetres wide so that the fold-over technique could be used to advantage. As illustrated in figure 3, each single warp thread is folded in half to provide two warp elements. In all commencement methods, the standard weft stroke used is the two-pair interlocking weft.

Another standard weaving stroke in all areas of Māori weaving is the single-pair twine, which was also used in the manufacture of eel traps (figure 4). With this weft stroke it was usual to space the rows apart (about one or two centimetres in kaitaka cloaks), hence the name 'spaced single-pair twine'. An examination of cloaks and capes, with the exception of dogskin cloaks, shows that spaced single-pair twining was a standard weave used in the main body of the garment. In superior cloaks the spacing of single-pair wefts was necessary to avoid stiffening the fabric; the warp threads were thoroughly beaten, washed and manipulated (kōmiri) by the hands in order to obtain a soft texture. This work would be nullified if the single-pair wefts were not spaced. In some cases, especially in the weaving of inner garments, such as are illustrated by Parkinson,[1] these may be as far apart as 15 centimetres.

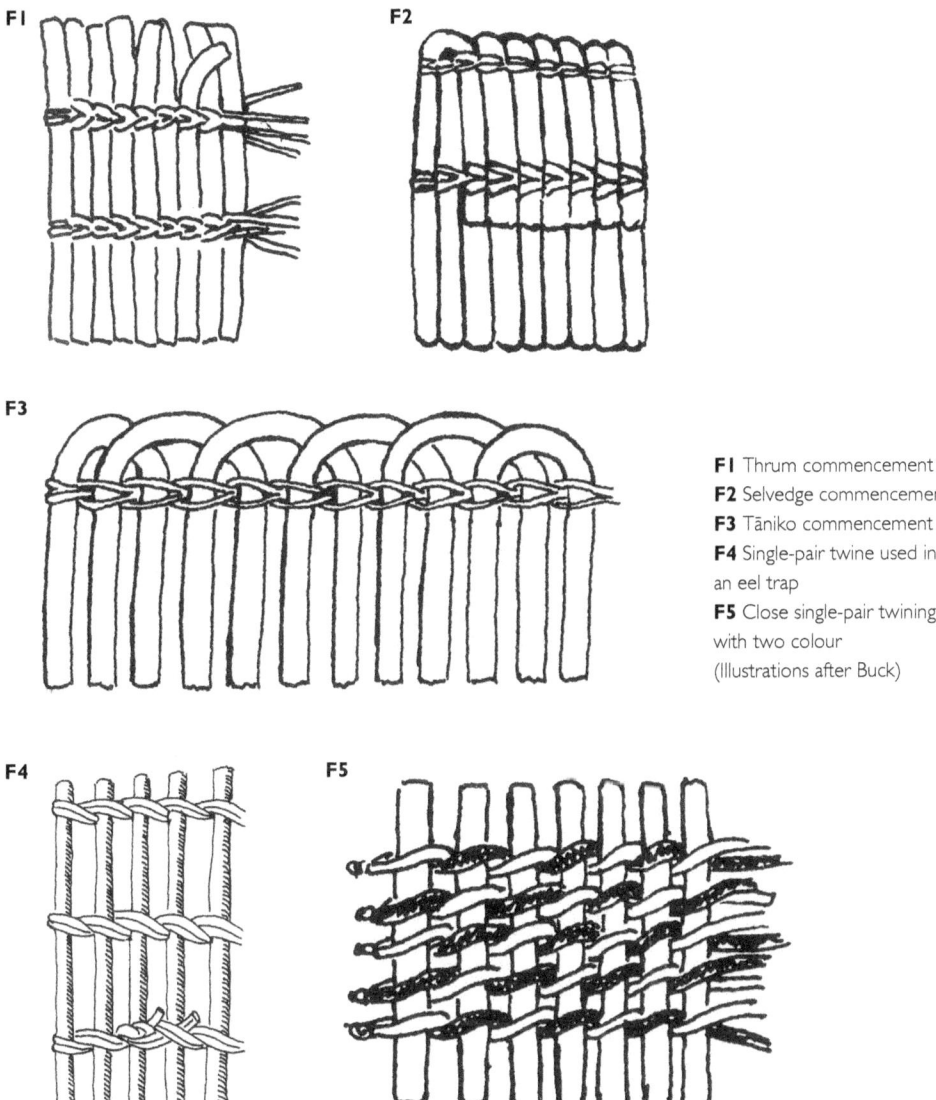

F1 Thrum commencement
F2 Selvedge commencement
F3 Tāniko commencement
F4 Single-pair twine used in an eel trap
F5 Close single-pair twining with two colour
(Illustrations after Buck)

When a stiff fabric was needed, such as for a war cloak (pukupuku) or a dogskin cloak, the single-pair twines were placed closely together. With the dogskin cloak, by so doing and by adding more fibre to both warp and weft elements, a foundation fabric, stiff enough to hold flat the strips of dogskin sewn on to it, was produced. The interesting thing about dogskin cloaks made this way is that they often had a simple tāniko border of about four rows in width, hidden under a fringe of dogskin and hair strips. This association of close single-pair twining and simple tāniko borders led Buck to believe that tāniko weaving developed out of dogskin cloak manufacture. However, the connection is not necessarily a technical one, and if it is, it is probably of a different order from technical evolution. Simple tāniko patterns on dogskin cloaks could be explained as custom or convention.

Although they were not visible, it was customary to have simple tāniko patterns on dogskin cloaks, covered by strips of hide. Side by side with such cloaks were others that featured elaborate tāniko patterns, so that it can be asserted that there is no strong case for establishing an evolutionary connection between close single-pair twining and the tāniko used on pūahi-type dogskin cloaks, that is, cloaks completely covered by strips of dog hide.

It is possible for technical knowledge to develop gradually, as existing techniques are improved by local experimentation or by borrowing ideas from elsewhere, or by flashes of insight as a new possibility is suddenly realised. There seems little doubt

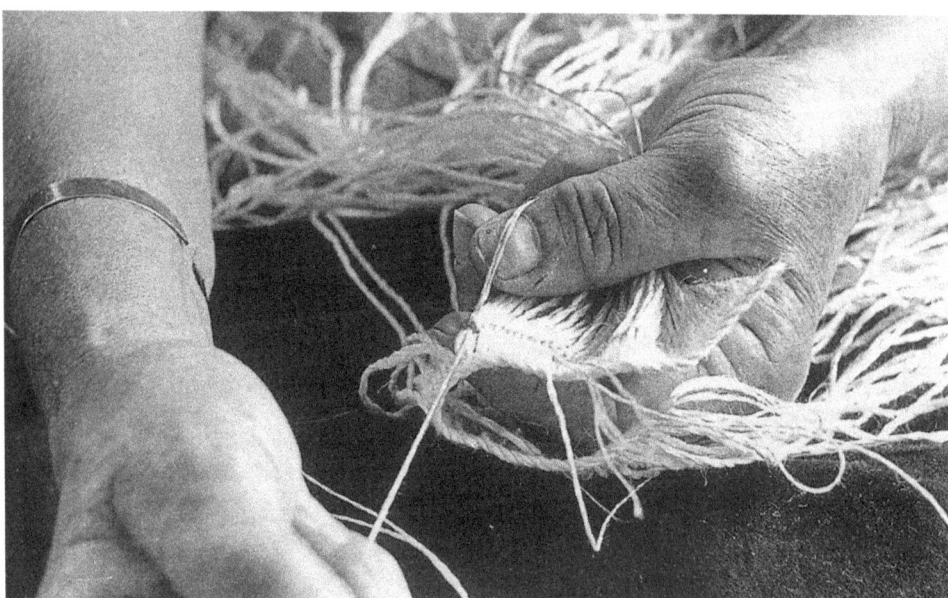

Plate 9 Mrs Rangimarie Hetet of Te Kuiti demonstrates how small tāniko work is held in the left hand and the threads manipulated by the right. The tāniko technique consists of a series of acquired motor habits that the student has to learn from a competent weaver.
C.A. Schollum

that the tāniko weave is a development of the single-pair twine. But who discovered it? Who made the breakthrough? Was it a long-term process or a discovery by insight? Was it an idea from central Polynesia? It is not a weaving tradition shared with other Polynesian groups, so therefore it must be a local development discovered by some enterprising weaver in New Zealand long before Captain Cook came on the scene.

It is conceivable that Māori weavers would have continued manufacturing cloaks and capes of many kinds for centuries without ever stumbling upon the tāniko weave. Had they been satisfied with a purely utilitarian article, no further inventions would have been required. Māori weavers, however, loved to decorate their cloaks, especially those worn by chiefs. The desire of chiefs to look resplendent and their wish to outdo others, combined with the technical and artistic skill of their weavers, meant there was always room for improvement and innovation.

There are logical steps that lead from the single-pair twine to the tāniko weave. The first developmental step is the use of two colours in each single pair weft row. Each row produces alternating colours (figure 5), and if these are arranged carefully, it is possible to produce several patterns — one of alternating oblique lines, another of alternating vertical lines — without changing the single-pair twine technique. But the pattern possibilities are strictly limited, so that if the weaver wanted patterns other than horizontal, oblique or vertical lines, a change in the technique was necessary. If she wanted a colour arrangement of three whites, seven blacks, three whites, seven blacks, how could she achieve it?

The solution was to develop the single-pair twine one stage further, so as to give the weaver complete control over colour arrangements. Technically speaking, the single-pair twine consists of a series of single rotations of the right wrist of the weaver, with no variation whatever. How the wrist is rotated depends on standardised methods of holding the work and manipulating the threads. By training, these become fixed motor habits (plate 9). To understand what is meant by a rotation of the wrist it is necessary to consult chapter eight which illustrates how the threads are secured. The weft threads are held as in Position One (page 107).

To execute the single-pair twine, the wrist is rotated in the direction in which the forefinger is pointing, as far as the wrist joint will allow. This point is illustrated by Position Two (page 107). By rotating the wrist in this manner, the white weft thread, which was at the bottom at the commencement of the movement, is now at the top. The next warp thread is inserted and the fingers are arranged in Position One again, with the black thread at the bottom. A twist of the wrist alters the position of the black thread to the top.

To return now to the first movement, that is, the rotation that brought the white weft to the top: supposing the fingers were withdrawn and arranged once more in Position One and the wrist were rotated again, the white weft would be back in the bottom position. This is really the secret of tāniko weaving. It is a weaving technique that uses one rotation of the wrist to change colour, and two rotations to use the same colour again. Such a technique enabled weavers to use up to four colours per row, and to change colour at will, thus enabling the construction of fairly complicated patterns. It can be seen, therefore, that tāniko is not radically different from the single-pair twine and could have been discovered by experimentation.

Buck arrived at the same conclusion in 1926, but he was prepared to be much more specific about which single-pair twine than I am. He wrote: 'We feel convinced that the wrapped twine technique of the Maori was derived from the single-pair twine of the coloured border of dogskin cloaks... and therefore tāniko work is an excellent example of independent evolution in New Zealand.'[2]

The trouble with this theory, however, is that it pins the development of tāniko to dogskin cloaks, whereas logically the discovery could have been made in any garment that was made with single-pair twining; thus it could have developed from capes. Then again, it is quite possible that tāniko weaving was discovered long before the pūahi type of dogskin cloak was invented. Recent evidence published by Stig Ryden on the Banks Collection points to a great antiquity for tāniko weaving, but of a different style from that commonly known. I shall discuss this early style in more detail later.

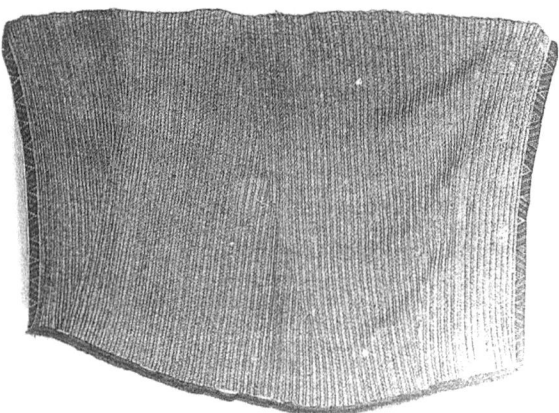

Cloak 1505 and detail below.

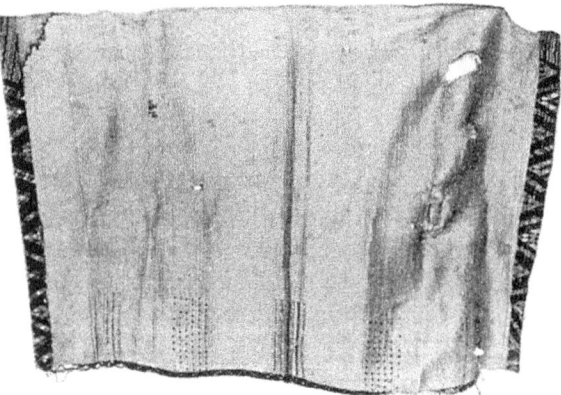

Cloak 29460 and detail below.

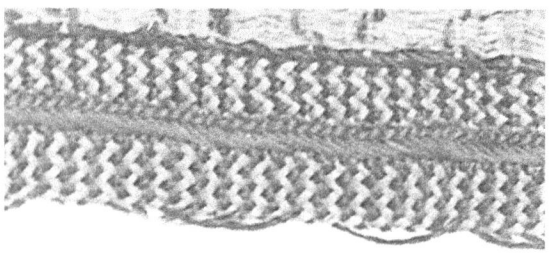

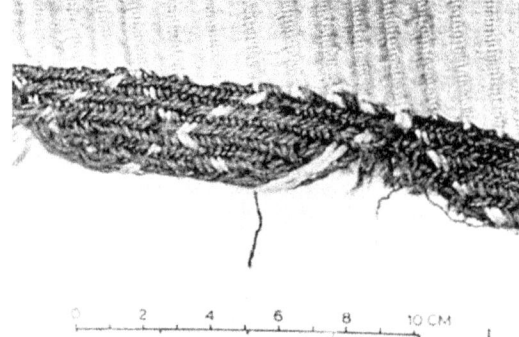

Plate 10 Plaited borders, which may have been the forerunners of tāniko weaving. A few early cloaks such as these from the Auckland Institute and Museum have a plaited band along the bottom border. C.A. Schollum

Recent research carried out by the author on the study of Māori cloaks held by the Auckland Institute and Museum indicates another possibility. A case can be established for a strong link between tāniko decoration and basketry techniques. It is highly probable that originally kaitaka cloaks were decorated with plaited borders such as are found on cloaks 1505 of the Sir George Grey Collection and 29460, a very old cloak placed on deposit in 1947. These plaited borders probably provided the models for patterns and for the direction tāniko weaving took. The antiquity of plaited borders is assured by a Banks specimen published by Stig Ryden. Plate 30 in Ryden's book features a Māori dogskin cloak, measuring 125 cm by 135 cm, of the pūahi type. On its lower hem it has 'a border in black resulting in something of a checker pattern on the side meant to be seen'.[3] A close examination of plates 30 and 35 in Ryden's book shows that this decorated strip is made in the same way as are the Auckland Museum cloaks 1505 and 29460.

Once the tāniko weave was discovered and perfected it was not very difficult to match and better the decorative possibilities of the plaited border. Tāniko had several advantages: more colours could be introduced, more complex patterns could be composed, and the decorative border could become an integral part of the cloak — not merely an addition sewn on. It was also softer against the skin. Structurally, tāniko possessed the supreme advantage of being manufactured of the same materials as the cloaks, thus warp elements of the same garments could also be used in the tāniko decoration. Tāniko weaving, therefore, could be the result of a deliberate application of cloak-making techniques to produce what were essentially basketry patterns. This is not just a wild stab in the dark, for a similar phenomenon has occurred in modern times. The tāniko technique is being rapidly replaced by the tapestry weave, but the patterns produced by the new method are the traditional tāniko patterns of old.

To conclude, I believe it can be said with reasonable assurance that tāniko weaving was a development from single-pair twining but that the model for pattern-making was provided by basketry. At one time decorative borders for cloaks were plaited and then attached to the body of the garment. Once tāniko weaving became known the same patterns that were used in the plaited borders were attempted with the new technique. The tāniko woven borders became fashionable, thus eventually replacing the older style. The cloaks shown in plate 10 show vestiges of this older style

Notes
1. Parkinson, 1773, plate XIX.
2. Buck, 1926, p. 227.
3. Ryden, 1963, p. 81.

4

The History and Development of Tāniko Weaving

It is possible to discuss the development of tāniko weaving from pre-contact days to the present without indulging in too much speculation, since documentary and artefactual evidence is available. For the sake of descriptive convenience the period is divided into three main stages:

Classical Māori period	AD 1650 to 1800
Transitional period	AD 1800 to 1900
Modern Māori period	1900 to present day

The Classical Māori period is characterised by the social, technological and artefact complex observed by Joseph Banks and James Cook when they visited New Zealand between 1769 and 1773. Artefacts they saw then were unaffected by contact with alien societies and therefore represent the end results of local developments to a technology that was originally eastern Polynesian in foundation. Furthermore, they represent the results of cultural responses and adaptations in a new environment to the physical and social needs of the Classical Māori. This period of long cultural isolation came to an end shortly after Cook's visits, so that the year 1800 is a fair point at which to fix the end of the Classical period.

From here on, contact with European traders, sealers, whalers, missionaries and settlers gradually increased, reaching the point of no return in the 1860s when the Māori were finally subdued by military action. By this time the land-hungry Europeans

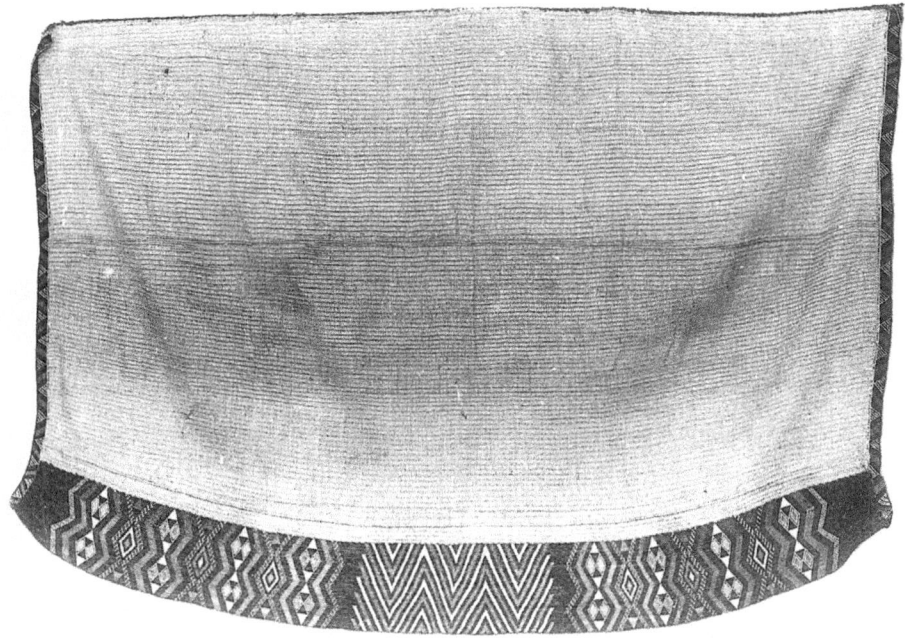

Plate 11 The pātea cloak, which has horizontal wefts in the main body of the garment and single tāniko borders on the side and bottom borders. Cloak 285E, Auckland Institute and Museum.

C.A. Schollum

were firmly entrenched and their hold over the country and the destiny of the Māori people tightened. I have called this crowded century the Transitional period because it was a time of profound and often painful change from the Classical Māori model to something quite different. It witnessed the change from the Māori's autonomy in his own land to minority status.

Although some startling changes have occurred in the Modern Māori period these are not of the same order as in the previous period. Changes here are a continuation of the adjustments that have to be made in a mixed ethnic social environment that is itself continually changing. It is thus impossible to envisage a time when no more changes are required because all the problems have been resolved. Human beings always have problems to solve and adjustments to make.

In the first two periods it is not possible to discuss tāniko as an isolated craft. Its history is intimately connected with cloak manufacture. It was a special form of decoration for the more distinguished garments.

The Classical Māori period

In attempting to describe what has happened to tāniko through the passage of time it is necessary to establish a baseline. Such a base is the Classical Māori period. Ethnographic descriptions and artefacts collected during this time help to provide the background information. Even though archaeologists have been very active and have been able to push back the arrival date of Māori to New Zealand to well beyond the year 1350, there is insufficient evidence available — in the case of clothing none at all — to form a starting point for discussion.

The Māori left their homeland some 700 years ago. They came from eastern Polynesia, an area where tapa cloth was made and where the aute (paper mulberry) tree flourished. Traditions say that the early Māori brought with them to the new land the sweet potato, the dog and, among other things, the aute tree. They tried hard to cultivate the aute but it would grow only in the warmer regions at the very northern end of New Zealand. They also tried hard to continue the manufacture of tapa cloth but both this and the cultivation of the tree were difficult to maintain in an environment so different from tropical Polynesia. That the tree was still being cultivated in 1769 against all odds points to the remarkable persistence of some cultural traits. In December 1769 while in the Bay of Islands, Banks observed a small stand of aute trees. This is what he recorded in his journal:

> After this they shewd us a great rarity, 6 plants of what they called Aouta from whence they made cloth like the Otahite cloth; the plant provd exactly the same, as the name is the same, as is usd in the Islands (Morus papyrifera Linn.) The same plant as is usd by the Chinese to make paper. Whether the climate does not well agree with it I do not know, but they seemd to value it very much and that it was scarce among them I am inclind to believe, as we have not yet seen among them pieces large enough for any use but sticking in to the holes of their Ears.[1]

Here is our evidence that tapa technology was still being maintained by the Classical Māori, but so little cloth could be manufactured from the limited sources that it acquired tremendous value as an ear ornament. Since tapa had become a scarce commodity it could hardly be used for clothing and new weaving material had to be found to fill this particular need. In the new land were ample stands of native flax of several varieties, which the early settlers exploited successfully. The results of exploitation and experimentation was first observed by Tasman in 1642 and then in more detail by Banks and Cook in 1769. A wide range of garments, including cloaks, kilts, aprons, capes, girdles and belts, all made of flax, were in use. Cook had this to say about the clothing he observed:

> Their common clothing are very much like square thrum'd mats... these they tie round their necks the thrum'd side out and are generally large enough to cover the body as low as the knee.... Besides these... they have much finer clothing made of the same plant... of this they make pieces of cloth about 5 ft long and 4 broad ... it is all work'd or made by hand.... To

one end of every piece is generally work'd a very neat border of different colours of four or six inches broad and they very often trim them with pieces of dogskin or bird feathers.[2]

Cook and Banks observed the whole range of Māori clothing, with the exception of war aprons, used by the Classical Māori. They observed also the application of tāniko on decorative borders, as the above passage makes clear.

However, this passage is a description of maximal dress. Māori did not always go around fully dressed. Cook reported that often the only clothing worn by the men was a belt around the waist 'to which is generally fastened a small string which tye round the Prepuce. In this manner I have seen hundreds of them come off to and on board the ship.[3] In the same report he described what the women wore. They wore secured around the waist a short thrummed cloak reaching 'as low as their knees'. He noticed that some women wore as their only covering a bunch of sweet-scented kāretu grass tied on with a piece of finely plaited cordage. When fully dressed they wore another thrummed cloak over their shoulders. The girdle, which I believe all adult women wore, was described thus by Banks:

> Round their waists instead of a belt they constantly wore a girdle of many platted strings... into this were tuckd the leaves of some sweet scented plant fresh gathered which like the fig leaf of our first mother servd as the ultimate guard of their modesty.[4]

As a convenient summary I shall describe briefly the minimum and maximum outfits of clothing considered to conform to the dress conventions of the Classical period and based on ethnographic descriptions from the Cook expeditions.

Minimum dress
For men: belt, and penis string.
For women: a girdle with a bunch of sweet-scented grass over the pubic area. Cook observed that very few women were actually dressed this way and Banks added that they were rarely without a garment around the waist. As part of women's minimal wear, therefore, we must add either a rāpaki (a cloak belted around the waist) or a piupiu which Banks described as 'a girdle of many platted strings'.

Maximum dress
For men: a rāpaki around the waist and a cloak or cloaks around the shoulders reaching well below the knee. The cloaks were of the kaitaka class generally, the korowai class less generally; the dogskin or red-feathered cloaks (kahu kura) were for men of rank. For women: a girdle, a rāpaki or piupiu around the waist, and a cloak or cape draped over the shoulders.

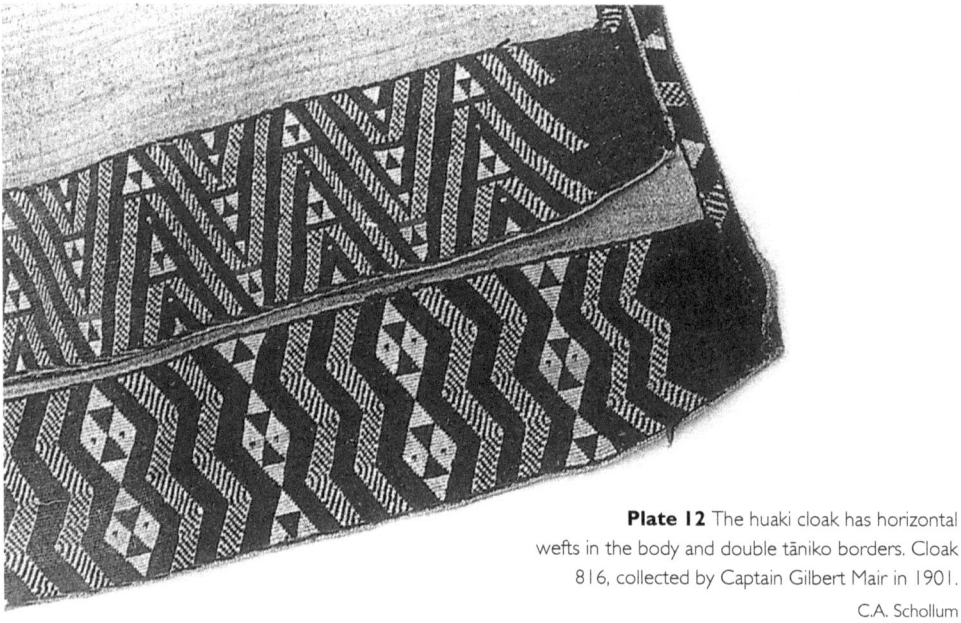

Plate 12 The huaki cloak has horizontal wefts in the body and double tāniko borders. Cloak 816, collected by Captain Gilbert Mair in 1901.
C.A. Schollum

Part of full costume consisted of body ornamentation in the form of permanent tattoo — full facial and buttock tattoo for men of proven fighting ability, and chin and lip tattoo for women of rank. Chiefs would have their hair done up in a topknot and just behind this they would place a decorative comb. Into the topknot would be placed two or three white gannet feathers. Ear ornaments consisted of tufts of tapa cloth, or greenstone pendants, or feathers, or human and shark teeth. Favourite neck ornaments were the greenstone tiki, the reiputaa (whalebone ornament), or necklaces of teeth or feathers, or of black irregular tubes.

Tāniko ornamentation is part of maximum costume, lending colour, pattern and extra grandeur to the total complex. Now that tāniko has been placed with in its cultural context for this period we can begin to examine the classes of display cloaks that featured tāniko patterns.

Dogskin cloaks

The body of the dogskin class of cloak was made with the close single-pair twine to form a foundation upon which strips of dogskin could be attached. Measuring anything up to an inch in width, the strips were placed vertically upon the woven body of the cloak and then secured in place by sewing, a bone needle being used for this purpose. The strip joins were concealed by the outside hair, which tended to give an impression of a continuous hide. Narrow tāniko borders were worked on the sides of these cloaks and sometimes on the neck borders. An example of a hairless variety of dogskin cloak that was collected by Banks is illustrated in plate 25. The technique of lacing the strips can be clearly seen in the photograph, and a part of the tāniko border is visible. As a rule, because the decorative borders were so narrow, the patterns appeared rather simple. A typical example may consist of four weft lines with which a pattern of alternating oblique lines of colour are worked.

Tāniko patterns in dogskin cloaks are usually so placed that they are concealed from view and therefore have no display function. This is very curious. That it was a matter of convention or custom is obvious, but why? Tāniko patterns may have had a ritual as well as aesthetic function formerly, or perhaps the tāniko technique, on technical grounds, provided a suitable finishing technique for this type of cloak. Who knows?

Plain-body cloaks (kaitaka)

A class of cloaks that has the main body left plain but the sides and bottom border decorated with tāniko patterns is generally known as kaitaka or parawai. A convention here was that tāniko was never applied to the neck border. The point needs emphasis owing to the practice adopted by early photographers and artists of posing Māori subjects in kaitaka cloaks worn upside down. Their reason for doing so is obvious enough, but the result is misrepresentation of ethnological facts.

The omission of body ornamentation such as feathers, strips of dogskin, tags and thrums resulted in the highlighting of tāniko patterns in this class of cloak.

From an artistic point of view this can be considered sound aesthetic judgement because the tāniko borders did provide sufficient ornamentation on their own. Any additional decoration on the body of the cloak would have detracted from the impact of the patterns. Such restraint in the application of decoration to clothing articles, and even to wooden artefacts, can be claimed as a characteristic of this period.

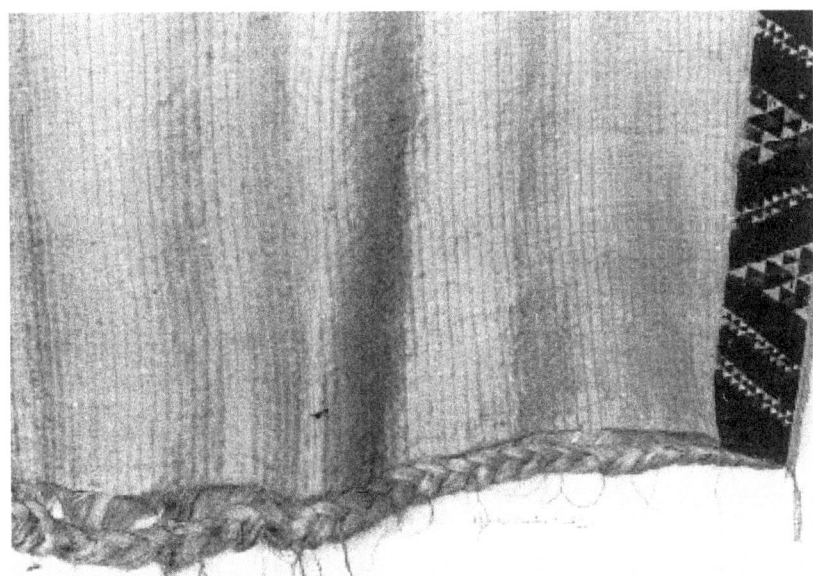

Plate 13 This unfinished cloak in the Auckland Collection illustrates the construction of a paepaeroa in which the body wefts are vertical. Cloak 7380. C.A. Schollum

Technically speaking there are two main types of kaitaka cloaks. In the first type the weft lines in the main body of the cloak run horizontally, and in the second the weft lines are vertical. The difference is not very obvious but is nevertheless an important one in manufacturing technique. The first type is begun at the neck border and is finished on one of the side borders; the other is begun from a side border and finished at the bottom tāniko border. If we disregard this technical difference and consider only the amount of tāniko decoration a further two varieties of kaitaka may be distinguished. One variety has single borders of tāniko and the other has double borders. There are thus four varieties of kaitaka cloaks.

1. Patea (cloak with horizontal weft and single tāniko borders). This variety has either only one tāniko border, which is along the bottom, or it has single borders along the sides and bottom. The neck border is the commencement edge. Though it is not actually made in the Classical period, cloak 285E, illustrated in plate 11, illustrates the type. The texture of the cloak may be judged by the fact that in the body there are 13 wpi (warps per inch), 20 wpi on the side border, and 26 in the lower tāniko border.

2. Huaki (cloak with horizontal wefts and double tāniko borders). The huaki looks like a double version of the pātea. The example featured here, cloak 816 in plate 12, was not made in the Classical period but serves to illustrate the type. The side borders are 2 centimetres wide, the outer bottom border is 15 centimetres wide and the inner one is 12.5 centimetres at its widest part. Texture measurements are 17 wpi in the body, and 23 wpi in the tāniko borders.

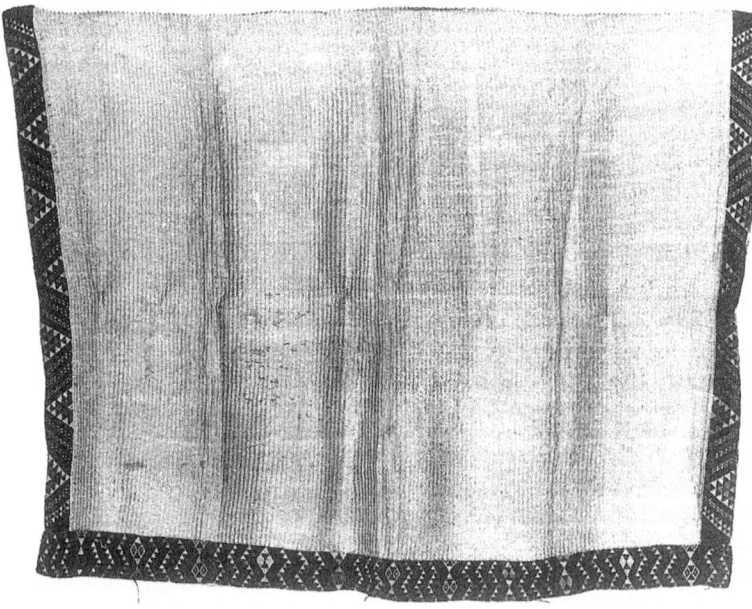

Plate 14 A completed paepaeroa cloak showing the single tāniko borders in position. Cloak 5567E, Auckland Institute and Museum
C.A. Schollum

3. Paepaeroa (cloak with vertical wefts and single tāniko borders). The paepaeroa is a vertical weft version of the pātea. The commencement edge may be either side. In the example used here, cloak 7380 in plate 13, the commencement edge is on the right. The suspension thread used to hang the work between two weaving pegs can be seen in the photograph.[5] The beginning edge could well have varied according to whether the weaver was left or right handed.

4. Paepaeroa-huaki (cloak with vertical wefts and double tāniko borders). This is a vertical weft counterpart of the huaki. The example featured here, cloak 1503 in plate 15, is from the Sir George Grey Collection and was most certainly made in the Transitional period. It is used here purely for illustrative purposes. The cloak, probably made for a child of rank, is 117 centimetres wide and 71 centimetres deep.

A strong possibility exists that both double-bordered kaitaka cloaks may in fact be developments of the Transitional period and examples of the efflorescence of tāniko during this time. They are included in this classification of kaitaka cloaks with the above caution. There seems little reason, however, to doubt the huaki in plate 12.

We have now described the range of clothing used by the Classical Māori and we have looked at the classes of cloaks that featured tāniko as a method of ornamentation. Māori weavers possessed the necessary body of technology together with the skills required for the manufacture of any garment within this range. The tāniko technique had been fully worked out as a method of decorating cloaks and adding to their display value. There appeared to be definite conventions regarding the application of tāniko. Such conventions make up the prevailing fashions, which limited not only the places

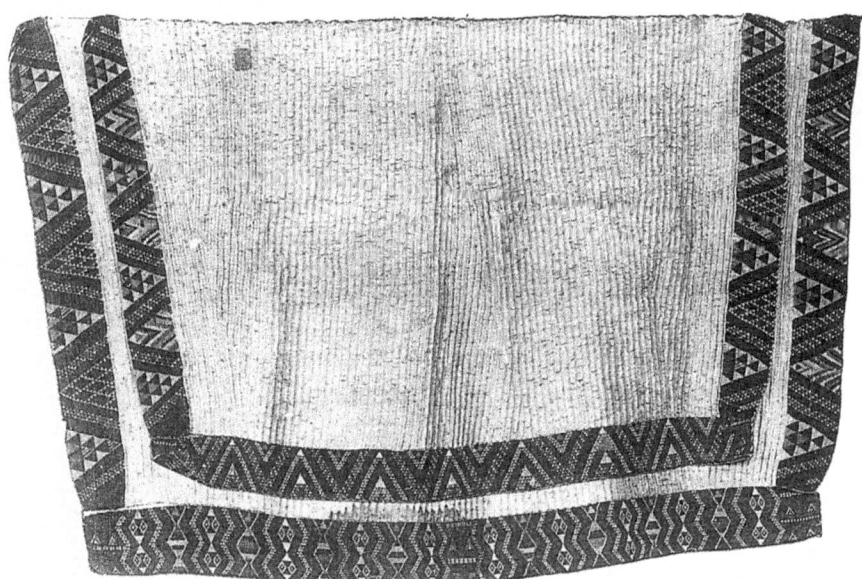

Plate 15 An illustration of the paepaeroa-huaki, in which body wefts are vertical and the sides and bottom are decorated with double tāniko borders. Cloak 1503, Auckland Institute and Museum. C.A. Schollum

where tāniko could be applied but also the choice of patterns, the size of the borders and the colours used. Furthermore, fashions had to operate within the bounds of accepted style whether it be tāniko, wood carving, hairstyle or fish-hook style. Thus there is a close relationship between fashion and style, the former being but one aspect of the latter.

A full discussion of stylistic features of tāniko patterns made in the Classical Māori period will be found in chapter five. The record points to the fact that there were two tāniko styles extant at the time of Cook; one was in its dying stages, and the other had become fashionable. Each style had its own characteristic way of combining motifs and each had its own colour preferences.

To summarise this section we have described the results of efforts made by the Classical Māori to adapt to a new environment; to exploit new sources of raw materials; to create a range of clothing that was warm, elegant and socially differentiated; and to extend their technology to meet new needs.

The Transitional period

The early decades of this period brought far-reaching changes in the social order of the Māori, who passed out of the Classical Māori era and the Stone Age during this time. Never again would he return to the old world — the Garden of Eden, the idealised paradise of the modern Māori. Early in the nineteenth century Europeans began to trickle in to the land rediscovered by Cook. Whalers, sealers, traders, escaped convicts and renegades of various nationalities began to arrive. The adventurous came first, followed by missionaries and later by permanent settlers. All of these people gave glimpses to the Māori of a different way of life, a different technological level, and an altogether strange and confusing set of values. Such changes as occurred in Māori society during this time of initial contact were organisational rather than structural. New ideas and things were simply assimilated into the old framework, and there were even efforts made to integrate stray Europeans into the Māori social system.

However, the trickle soon became a steady flow, and then a torrent, as settlers began to pour into the country. There were now far too many Europeans to be integrated into the Māori system, and in 1858 the point of no return was reached when the population of settlers passed that of the indigenous people. By and large the settlers were not interested in integrating the Māori people into their way of life. This could be left to government agencies and the missionaries. The settlers' goal was ridiculously simple: they wanted the Māori to move over for them. Desperation eventually drove the Māori to warfare against European settlers and the government. The Taranaki War of 1860 and the Waikato Campaign of 1863 resulted in disastrous defeat not only of the tribes taking part in the conflict but, in a sense, of the whole of Māoridom. They became a humiliated and humbled people and many became embittered over the unjust reprisals taken against them. This, then, became a period of very serious adjustment to a situation over which the Māori had little control. Important structural changes occurred — leadership systems broke down, populations became decimated and some landless, the religious system was overthrown and the whole social fabric loosened. The greater part of the Classical technological inventory changed or disappeared. A new range of raw materials, artefacts and machinery made obsolete what the Māori was able to retain.

Western-type institutions of economics, politics, education, law and religion were introduced and adjustments had to be made if the Māori were to come to terms with them. New likes and dislikes came into the preference system, and so clothing fashions changed. European clothes had been adopted by the middle decades of the Transitional period, and by the end of that period the traditional range of Māori clothing had passed out of general use.

The social history of the period may be summarised thus: enthusiastic contact — clash — withdrawal — reorientation. In material culture the story runs: contact — trial — acceptance of the new — rejection of the old.

The range of clothing

From 1769 onwards, Europeans introduced into New Zealand an entirely new range of clothing, which was even worn in a different way: where Māori clothes were wrapped around the body, European clothes were designed to be climbed into. There were shirts, trousers, socks, shoes or boots, hats and waistcoats for men; and pretty long frocks and dresses, petticoats, drawers, bonnets, stockings and shoes for the ladies. Initially, these garments were little more than curiosities that did not change Māori basic clothing fashions. The French explorer Jules Dumont d'Urville visited Tasman Bay in the South Island on 16 January 1827 and this is what he saw:

> These savages seemed to know about firearms, but very little about iron or instruments made of this metal, for they did not value anything but materials. They had not brought weapons of any kind with them and their cloaks were all made of reed or coarse straw of New Zealand flax (*Phormium tenax*) except one, which was of fine silky material made of blue cotton, after refusing to give it in exchange for some excellent axes and even a sword.[6]

What the explorer thus reported may be regarded as fairly typical of most of the coastal villages, and it is evident that a demand for European clothes was astir by as early as 1827. Thirteen years later Dumont d'Urville returned to New Zealand, and he noticed at once the effects of contact with Europeans upon the Māori. Writing about the Māori of Otago Harbour, whom he saw in 1840, he said:

These men were the same type of New Zealanders whom I had seen on my earlier voyages, but they had certainly not gained by the contact with whalers. As a rule they were dressed in European fashion: this costume, which did not really hide their dirty condition, made them look like beggars covered in rags; they were revolting; they appeared to have abandoned the old spirit of independence and those warlike qualities, which on my first voyage had seemed to be peculiarly characteristic of the race.... No trace of any skilled industry was to be found; the cloaks of Phormium (flax) have been replaced by woollen garments from Europe; the inhabitants of Otago seem to have given up the primitive dress which suited them so well.[7]

Although this account may seem overdramatic, it does give a clear impression of the startling changes that had occurred in a short time. By 1840 the coastal tribes in contact areas had adopted European clothing fairly extensively. It took a little longer for inland tribes to acquire enough of the new things to satisfy their needs. It was only a question of time, however, before all Māori tribesmen would outfit themselves with new clothes, for such is the way of fashion. By the close of the 1800s the changeover was complete.

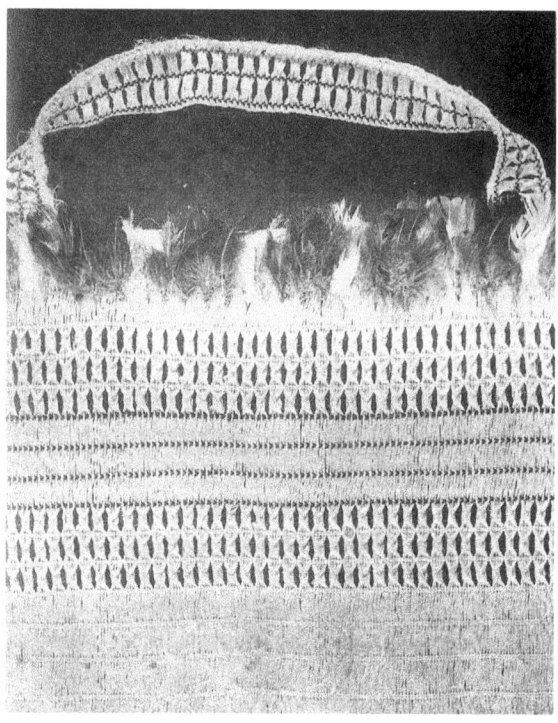

Plate 16 A bodice (pari) first introduced into Māori costume during the Transitional period. Cloak-making techniques were used in this example made for Mrs Joy Biggs by Mrs Te Kanawa of Te Kuiti. Early bodices were made with the same techniques but were modelled on blouses.

C.A. Schollum

European clothes had been adopted for the functions of protecting the body, of satisfying the new moral code, and of keeping up with a new clothes fashion. The traditional range began to take on a new function, that is, as ceremonial costume.

Experimentation was a feature of this period. New clothes were tried out, sometimes with comical results; for example, shirts were often worn as trousers and stockings as shirtsleeves. The combination of garments worn by some Māori not familiar with European dress style often offended the European's sense of propriety because the fundamentals of the style were being violated. Blankets were bought as substitutes for cloaks and for a time these were more popular than coats, but the longer the period of contact the more surely European clothing style dominated.

Over a century of contact was necessary to bring about the complete adoption of European clothing style. Meanwhile, several things happened to the traditional range; much of it was bought by explorers, curio hunters, museum collectors and the more affluent settlers. A large quantity was presented to important civic and government officials as a symbol of goodwill and peace. Sir George Grey's Collection, for example, was built up in this way. Very many articles were buried with their owners. Such material as remained was kept as heirlooms or as ceremonial costume.

Production was greatly reduced as the population declined and as European clothes became easily available. Now that the ceremonial function alone was important, it was possible to select from the range those articles that best served ceremonial purposes; the rest were allowed to disappear. For example, from the wide variety of piupiu and capes only one variety was retained; and with cloaks, the dogskin and kaitaka varieties had passed out of existence by the end of the period.

But with costume it was not simply a question of deleting unsuitable garments from the range; some additions were also necessary. Women's breasts had now to be covered, and so the bodice (pari) was introduced as a necessary part of female costume. Drawers and underskirts for women and shorts for men became mandatory. The tāpeka modelled on the leather bandoliers of British troops became a part of male ceremonial attire. Thus, in this period of tremendous change, a solution had been worked out and one which was adjusted to the new social situation.

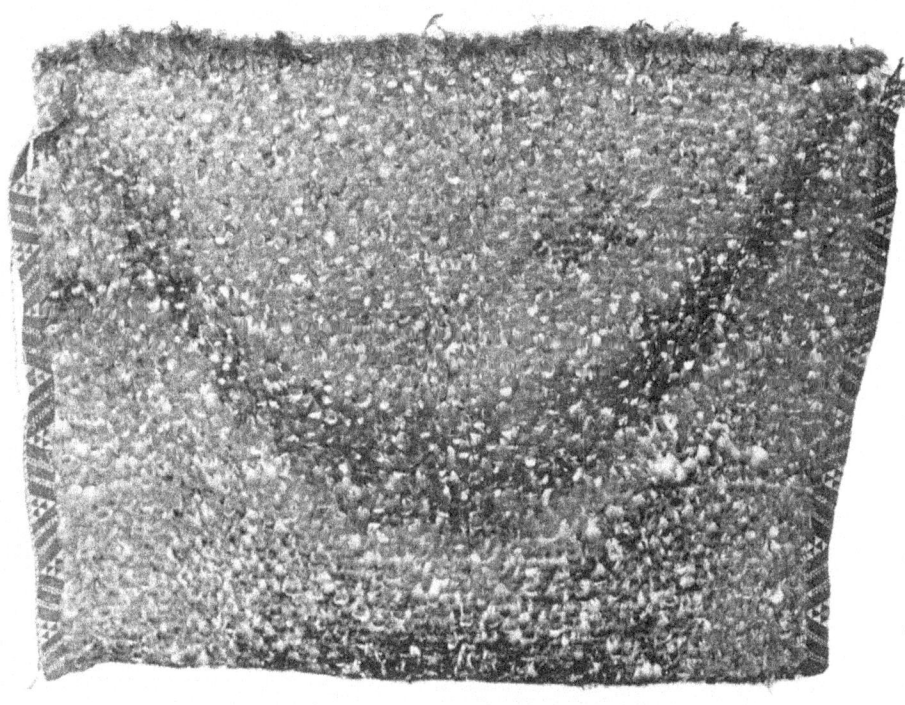

Plate 17 A feather cloak with tāniko borders, made in the Transitional period. Texture measurements are 26 wpi in the borders and 10 wpi in the body. The wefts in the cloak are spaced at 15 mm intervals. Auckland Institute and Museum.
C.A. Schollum

Changing fashions in Māori clothing style

One of the earliest signs of contact is marked by the introduction of wools of assorted colours into cloaks and kilts. At first these were oversewn onto old garments both in the body of the garment and in the tāniko borders. Later, the entire weft material of tāniko patterns consisted of wool. According to Angas, the women obtained their wool by purchasing blue and scarlet caps, and 'variegated comforters' from the traders.[8] These articles were unpicked by the women and the wool used as decorative elements in cloaks and kilts.

This early phase is also marked visually by the addition of colours beyond the usual Classical range of reddy-brown, black or dark brown, white and yellow. The patterns were worked in blue, green, turquoise, purple, scarlet and wool white, which is different from the white of bleached flax fibre. The pattern motifs used, however, continue to be within the Classical range, and the main body of cloaks, capes and kilts were made in flax fibre by traditional techniques. The main changes in fashion for the first half of the Transitional period are the features mentioned above, which are comparatively minor.

In the next half of the period greater changes occurred. The earlier conventions regarding where decorations should be applied and in what quantities, broke down. Restraint in decoration went by the board. Formerly cloaks such as the kaitaka,

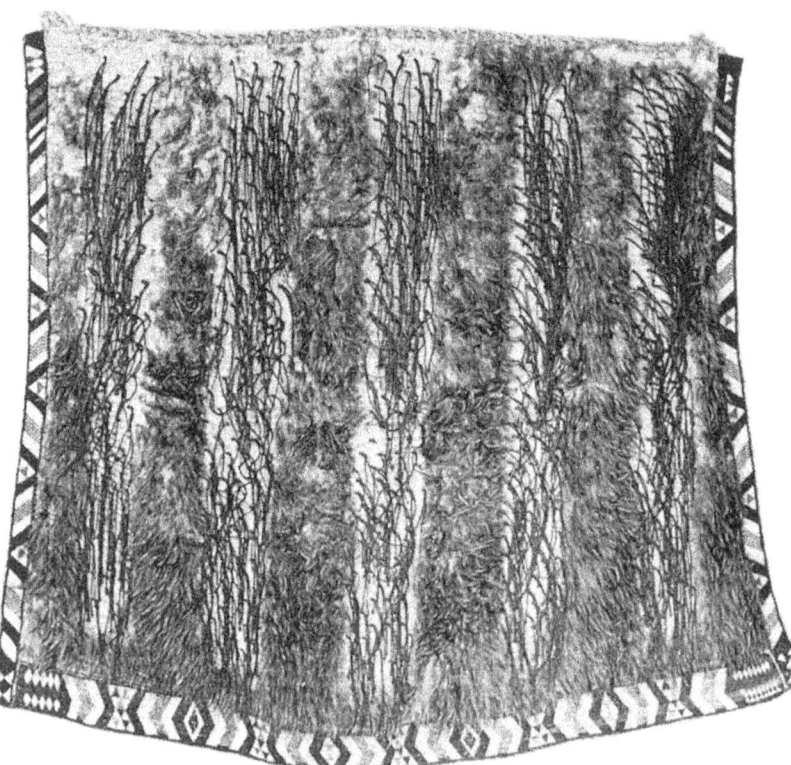

Plate 18 This cloak was made early in the Modern period by Mrs Rangimakehu Hall of Utuhina, Rotorua. It illustrates the intermixture of korowai, kaitaka and kahu huruhuru cloak types, a trend begun in the Transitional period. Cloak 20682, Auckland Institute and Museum.
C.A. Schollum

korowai and kahu huruhuru (feather cloaks) had been more or less mutually exclusive classes, each type being decorated in a predictable way. Korowai cloaks now became decorated with feathers as well as with the traditional thrums; feather cloaks became decorated with tāniko patterns (plate 17) instead of feathers only, and so on. There are also examples of cloaks that mix three classes in one: kaitaka, korowai and feather cloaks. Cloak 20682, plate 18, provides a good example.

A further marker of fashion is the extended application of tāniko beyond the traditional kaitaka class of cloak, together with the tendency for borders to become wider. Dogskin cloaks, however, passed out of the inventory completely and so in this area of tāniko application there was a loss. It is undeniable, however, that fashion changes of this period acted in favour of tāniko. For example, towards the very end of the period, and continuing into the next, tāniko patterns were applied to the waistbands of piupiu. An example is shown in plate 19.

Why tāniko should have continued to gain in popularity is an interesting question. A likely answer is that its persistence was because it was greatly valued by the Māori people themselves and encouraged by the European population. It seems reasonable that European prejudices would have had some influence in either perpetuating some

Plate 19 An old piupiu belonging to Mrs Ponga Chadwick of the Waikato-Maniapoto area. Made by an unknown weaver, the tāniko is of excellent quality and represents good Late Transitional and Early Modern work.
G.A. McCracken

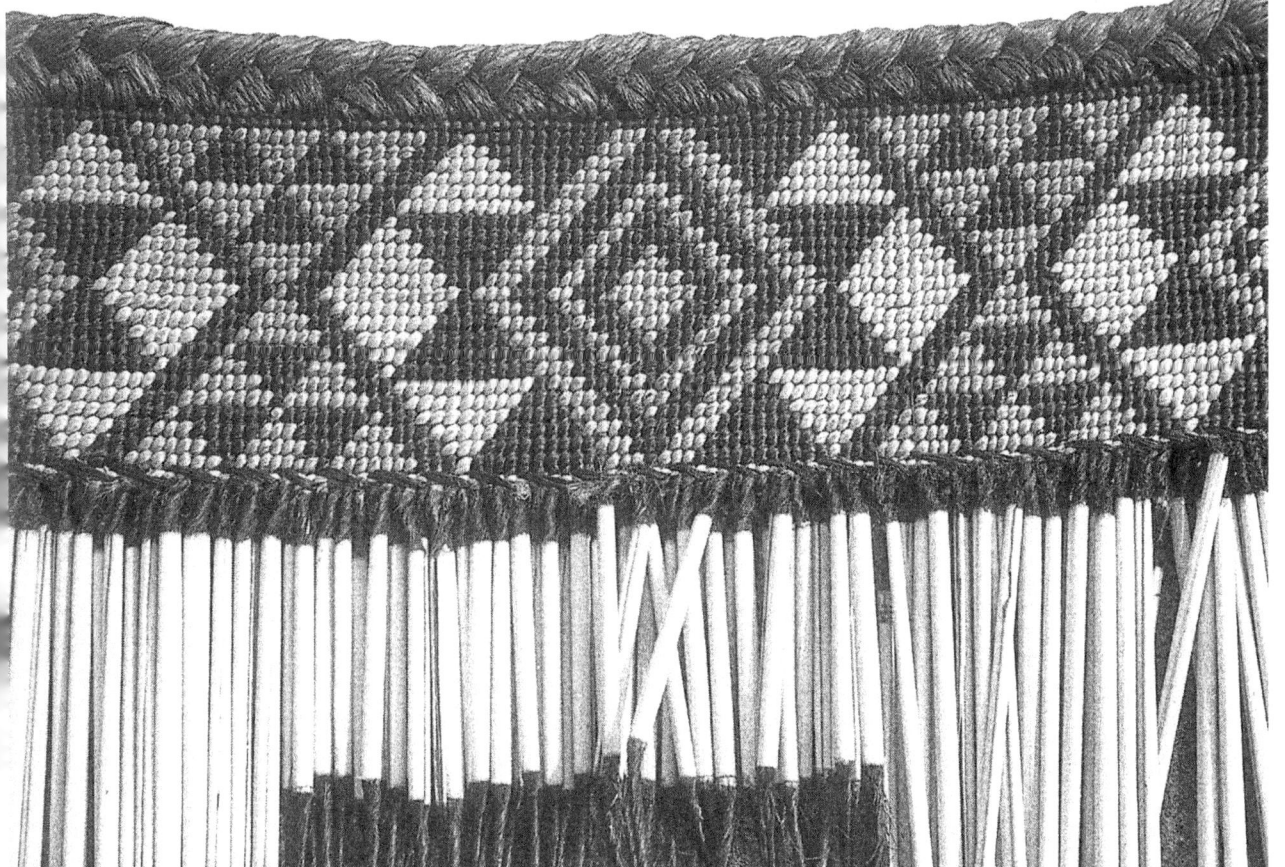

cultural trait or in hastening its extinction. Positive influence would have resulted from the purchase by Europeans of tāniko decorated articles. I suspect also that while other items of Māori material culture may have been devalued by missionary influence, for example, by being equated as works of the devil, tāniko escaped this because of its similarities to tapestry weaving, which is a familiar part of European culture. Tāniko as a craft and as an art activity could, therefore, be appreciated more readily by the European.

Technical changes

Contact with Western culture increased the range of materials Māori weavers could use in their work. Wool was the first such element seized on. Much later in the period embroidery cottons were tried out. The settlers introduced new animals and domesticated fowl into the country, and these, too, brought changes in Māori clothing. Cloaks decorated with peacock, pheasant and domestic hen feathers appeared. Twine and candlewick were also pressed into service. Most of these intrusive elements were used for decorative effect.

Cloaks that were made to be worn were constructed in such a way that they fitted over the shoulders and buttocks of the wearer. To accomplish this, the weaver wove in wedges — extra weft lines that allow for the body's bulges. Usually, there were two such wedges: one providing for the shoulder bulge; and the other for the buttocks. In the cloak illustrated in plate 20 the wedges can be seen by following the horizontal white weft lines. The first wedge is just above the halfway mark and the other is below it. Cloaks made as genuine wearing garments hang in a characteristic way and this important feature is illustrated in plate 20. As cloaks lost their primary function of everyday wear, weavers dispensed with the wedges until by the end of the period the technique was rarely used.

The enthusiasm for wool as a weaving material was short-lived. Wool deteriorated much more quickly than flax fibre, the colours faded after exposure to the weather, and wool was subject to attack by moths. On such utilitarian grounds it had to be rejected, as indeed it was towards the end of the period.

The tendency to increase tāniko borders has already been mentioned. Angas mentions that in some cases the decorative borders of kaitaka cloaks were 'a couple of feet in depth'.[9] No examples of cloaks with such wide borders ever found their way into the Auckland Collection, so perhaps Angas was exaggerating, but there are any number of cloaks that illustrate the tendency he first noted in 1844. That such a tendency continued into the Modern period is shown by the example illustrated in plate 21. The right-hand cloak is a feather cloak to which tāniko has been added as an extra ornamentation and illustrates the extent of tāniko elaboration.

It would appear that the emotional stress and strain of the period are reflected by a kind of corresponding turmoil in clothing decorative techniques. Aesthetic conventions are disrupted and restraint and strict adherence to style lapse. Restraint is not a characteristic of the period, either with Māori or with Europeans, so that its absence in decorative art should cause no surprise. With stylistic conventions upset, the artistic or creative spirit spills over beyond the traditional boundaries, and tremendous changes occur. This has been noticed before by students of style and fashion. For example, the American anthropologist A.L. Kroeber wrote: 'All that these sociopolitical tensions seem really to do, is to impart generic tension, upset, and instability to designers of fashion and to the audience and clientele that designers and purveyors serve.'[10]

In the case of tāniko, patterns become brighter and more elaborate. They are applied to a greatly increased field, and when the cloaks to which

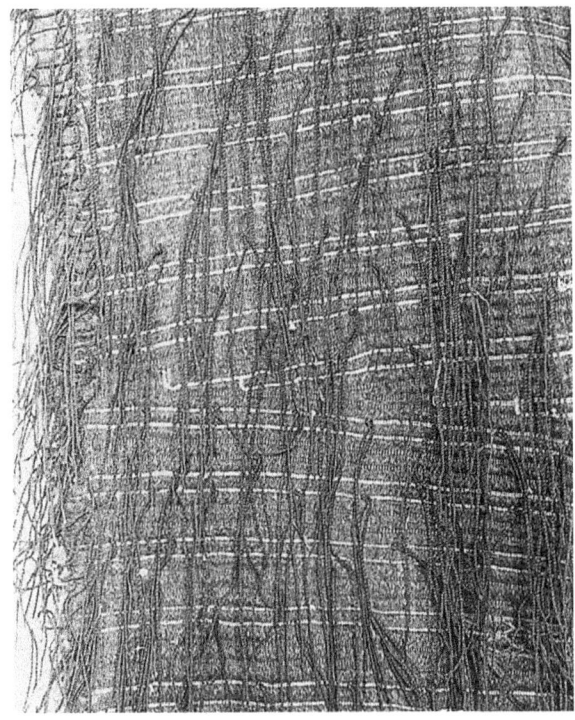

Plate 20 An unusual korowai acquired by the Auckland Museum in 1887. It is the only cloak in the entire collection that uses the idea of dyeing all the warp material of the body for added decorative effect. Undyed weft elements show up clearly and can be used to locate the two wedges which have been worked into the body to allow for the shoulders and buttocks of the wearer.
C.A. Schollum

tāniko was a bound form pass out of existence it survives and becomes established as an independent craft. It is an essential for the ceremonial costume which is all that is left of a once extensive range of traditional garments. The everyday scene is dominated by Western-style clothes. These are some of the results of the tension and instability mentioned by Kroeber. Changes of such magnitude, which result in the overthrow of styles and the acceleration of fashion changes, arise when the foundations of a society are not merely rocked but severely jolted.

The Modern Māori period

Even though difficult times were (and are yet to be) faced by the Māori people, the social problems of this period are nowhere near as cataclysmic as those which they faced in the Transitional period. At the beginning of the period the Māori is becoming more involved in the general life of a struggling nation. The 1929 Depression hits them

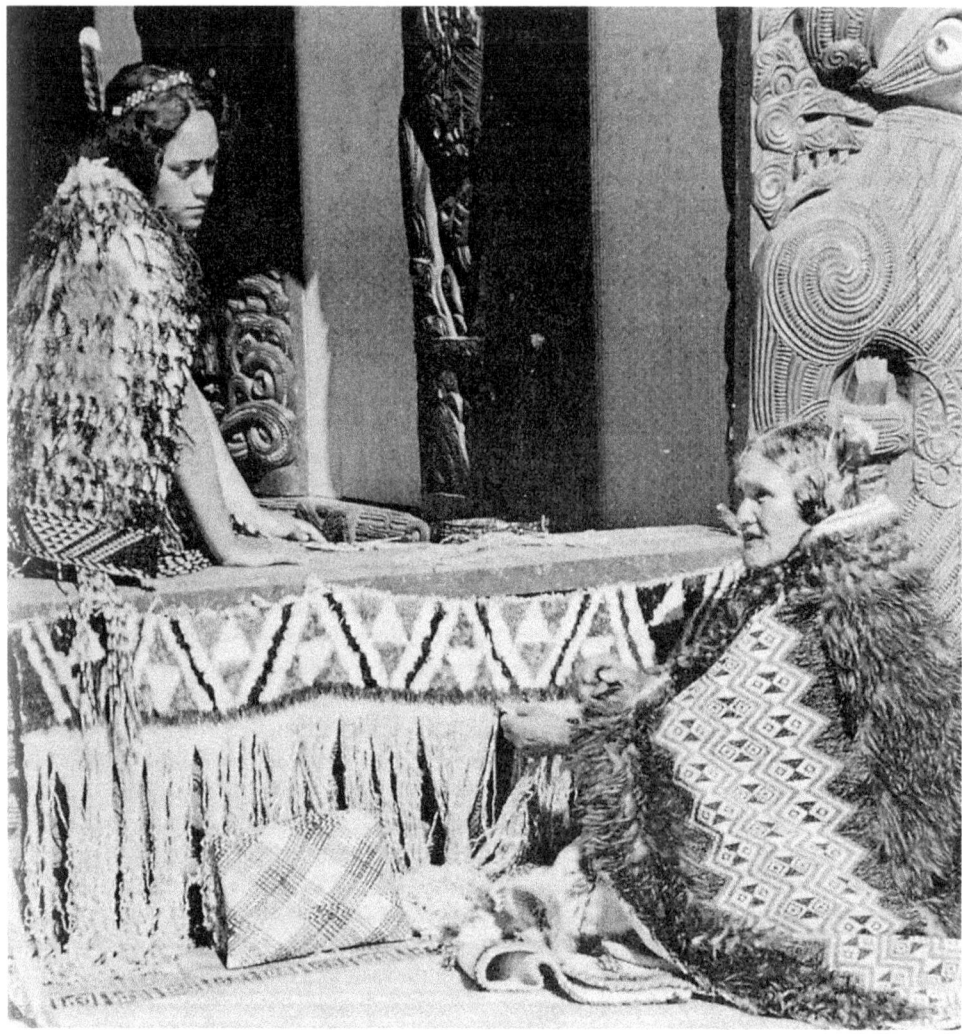

Plate 21 The cloaks in this photograph illustrate the tendencies to mix cloak classes, to apply tāniko decorations in areas not previously permitted, and to increase the size and width of tāniko ornamented areas. These cloaks were probably made early in the Modern period by Rotorua weavers.
National Publicity Studios

as hard as, or probably harder than, the European settlers, but they survive it. The Māori population of 1921 was 56,000 — a slight improvement on the all-time low of 42,000 in 1896.[11] The future held out some hope. The Young Māori Party represented by such giant figures as Sir James Carroll, Bishop Bennett, Sir Peter Buck, Tutere Wirepa, Hone Heke and Sir Apirana Ngata had been in existence since 1890,[12] and were doing a sterling job of interpreting New Zealand's brand of Western culture to the Māori people. In 1929 the New Zealand Government accepted the principle of using public funds to finance the development of Māori land, but the Depression prevented any large-scale operation.[13]

Changes in Piupiu Fashions

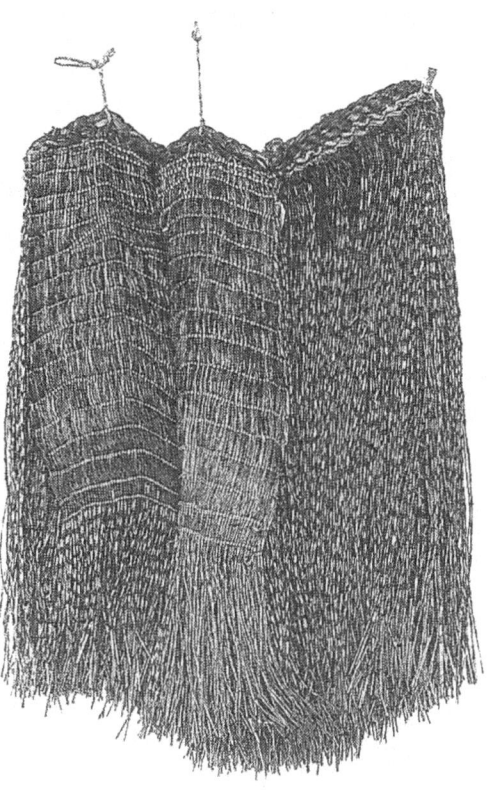

Plate 22A A kilt typical of the Classical period. The suspended strands consist of flax fibre dyed black and twisted into two-ply strings.

Plate 22B The inside view, showing that these garments were designed for warmth and protection. The main body is made like a cloak.

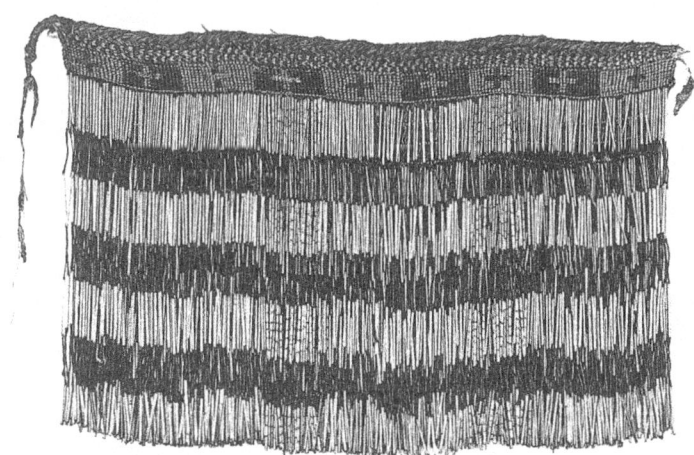

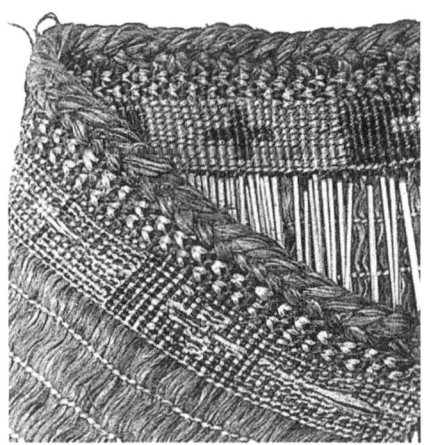

Plate 23A This kilt was made in the Transitional period. The cross in the tāniko band bears witness to the acceptance of Christianity. The outer decoration method is still popular today.

Plate 23B The inside view of the same kilt shows that the cloth area is still considerable and that the foundation of the garment is still Classical in conception.

Bodices, headbands and bandoliers still feature tāniko patterns, and old motifs are receiving more attention as the costume becomes more formalised. There is thus a tendency in modern fashions to return to traditionalism, but it is a tendency existing simultaneously with an opposite one of change.

Piupiu have become highly simplified in this period although still manufactured largely by traditional methods. The tubular strands have been reduced to but a single row, whereas it was double at the beginning of the period; the waistband became narrower in the 1960s, but during the 1990s the tāniko band became wider.

An outstanding feature of the period is the splitting of fashions into high and low. Cloaks made by traditional methods are used in high ceremonial, and impressionistic cloaks made by new techniques are relegated to use by entertainers. Weavers of the former tend to be women who have become very proficient in cloak-making over many years, while makers of impressionistic cloaks tend to be the young people who need them for their performing team.

Technical changes

It is in the field of technical changes that the most profound changes have occurred. The simplification of piupiu design has already been mentioned. The photographs shown in plates 22, 23 and 24 make abundantly clear the progression towards simplicity of design in this garment.

The same tendency towards simplicity is apparent in the cloaks used by entertainers, but it is of a slightly different order. Traditional materials and methods are used in piupiu but in the case of cloaks faster techniques are employed, and materials that can be readily purchased at a store and which have already been processed are used. Less man-hours are required to produce these cloaks, whereas even the simplified piupiu still takes several days.

Techniques used for the manufacture of bodices, bandoliers and headbands used to be based on tāniko. In 1946, when I first became interested in tāniko, these articles of costume were not very numerous. Those I saw then used macramé twine as warp material, or at times dyed twine or fishing line. Weft materials consisted of embroidery silks. Intrusive motifs, such as stars, fern leaves and trees, were rather popular. Many of the producers of that time were trained as pupils in Māori schools, so the Māori school system played an important role in the perpetuation of this craft, and of others.

In the next decade many weavers experimented with the tapestry technique for producing bodices, headbands and bandoliers. Some entertainment teams competed in costume made this way and were apparently not discouraged, because in the next decade tapestry became widespread. The tāniko technique, after nearly 200 years of contact, is finally displaced in popular fashions by a new technique that is a little easier to handle. With the new technique wool comes back into fashion, and this is the favoured material today. A piece of tapestry mesh forms the foundation of each article, and onto this the patterns are worked in wool. It has the distinct technical advantage of

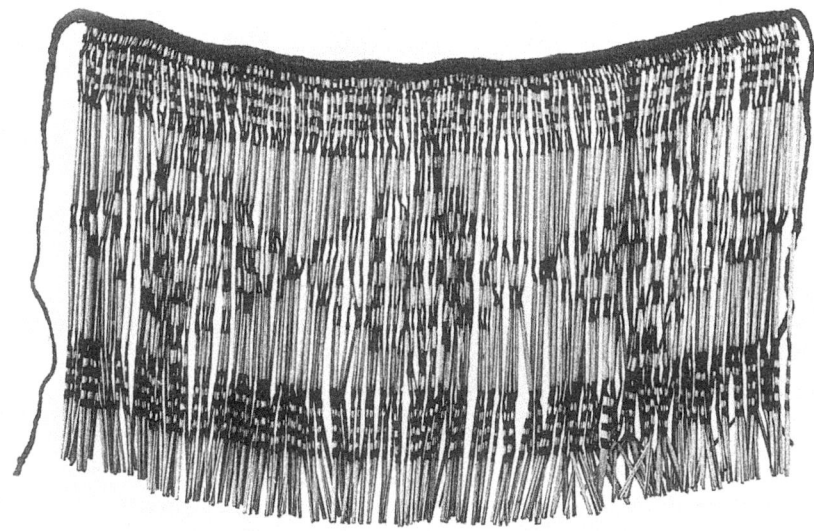
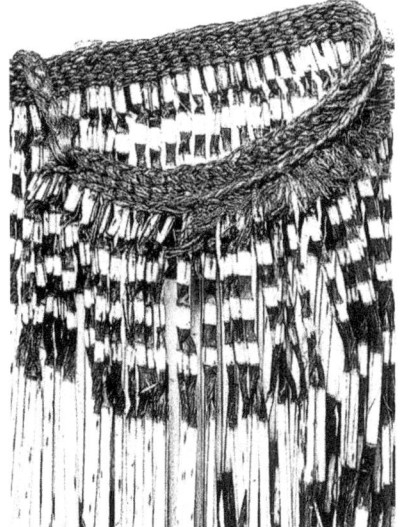

Plate 24A This is a modern kilt made by Mrs Raponi of Ngapuna, Rotorua. Its outer aspect is the same type of decoration as in the previous kilt.

Plate 24B This is a detail of the same kilt and it shows up the complete absence of cloth area on the inside. The waist attachment is reduced to a safe minimum sufficient to secure the suspended strands to the garment for as long as the kilt will last.

C.A. Schollum

setting the boundaries for the pattern within which the decorator can work. A further important advantage is that a novice can do tolerably well with a first effort, whereas with the tāniko technique the first effort is rarely a satisfactory piece of work and is usually hidden away or destroyed. Examples of tapestry worked tāniko patterns are shown in plate 1.

Conclusion

In this survey of the history and development of tāniko weaving we have seen how social and technological changes interweave with each other, and we have seen something of the way in which the factors of continuity and change operate.

A final point that I want to discuss here is the problem of what is most basic in an artefact, such as an article of costume. We know from this survey that the basis is certainly not its material aspect.

Trousers may be made in either tweed or dacron without causing any fundamental change; it is still a pair of trousers. We have seen also that the basis is not its technical aspect; a bodice is still a bodice whether it is made in tāniko or in tapestry. Similarly tāniko patterns are still tāniko patterns whether they are executed in tapestry or in the traditional weave.

We are thus left with nothing concrete to work on. What seems to linger is an idea in the mind, a notion of shape, form, function, cultural significance and sentiment. The Māori word āhua, denoting semblance, subsumes this conceptual aspect of an artefact; the āhua of tāniko persists in spite of the many changes it has undergone. In terms of culture the āhua, as defined above, is the most fundamental aspect of an artefact. It outlasts the real thing.

Basically, therefore, culture consists of ideas rather than of things. Such a view of culture, however, is not new. American archaeologist Paul S. Martin advanced practically the same idea in 1938. It was later made more explicit by Cornelius Osgood in 1940, and then really sharpened by another American archaeologist, Walter Taylor, in 1948.[15] By a process of deductive interference from the facts presented here, I find myself in the same camp as these scholars.

Notes

1 Beaglehole, 1962, Vol. 1, p. 444.
2 Beaglehole, 1955, p. 279.
3 Beaglehole, 1955, p. 279.
4 Beaglehole, 1962, Vol. 1, p. 16.
5 Buck, 1926, plate 26.
6 Wright, 1950, p. 75.
7 Wright, 1955, p. 17.
8 Angas, 1847, Vol. 1, p. 324.
9 Angas, 1847, Vol. 1, p. 323.
1 0 Kroeber, 1 963, p. 21.
1 1 Sinclair, 1959, p. 190.
1 2 Ramsden, 1948, pp. 35-36.
13 Sinclair, 1959, p. 265.
14 *Te Ao Hou*, 6, p. 18.
15 Martin (1938, p. 296) says culture is 'any system of conventional or traditional ideas as expressed in ways of doing things and making things'. Osgood (1940, p. 25) says, 'Culture consists of all ideas concerning human beings which have been communicated to one's mind and of which one is conscious.' Taylor (1948, p. 109) defines culture thus: 'By culture as a descriptive concept, I mean all those mental constructs or ideas which have been learned or created after birth by an individual.' Continuing with his two-part definition, he says (p. 110), 'By culture as an explanatory concept, I mean all those mental constructs which are used to understand, and to react to, the experiential world of internal and external stimuli.'

5

Style and Tāniko Patterns

A purely typological classification of tāniko patterns ignores, if not completely then to a considerable extent, the factor of time. All patterns are lumped together and then put into the various categories that appeal to the classifier. Another way of discussing patterns and imposing some order upon the material at hand is to use the concept of style. This concept, though familiar to students of archaeology and art alike, is nevertheless a very tricky one; style has different meanings for different people. At the outset, therefore, I must indicate what I mean by this term.

What has become a classic for many people is the definition given by Meyer Schapiro in 1953; he defined style as 'the constant form — and sometimes the constant elements, qualities, and expression — in the art of an individual or of a group'.[1] By this is meant that the work of one person or of a group such as the New Zealand Māori exhibits similarities of form, quality and expression, to a degree that an investigator would have little difficulty in recognising that the works belong to that individual or group. If the individual and the group can be recognised, it usually follows that the locality where the works were produced can be identified too. But the work of an individual or of a group does not remain the same through time. The constants change. For example, Picasso's earliest paintings are vastly different from his later creations. Similarly in tāniko, patterns produced in AD 1700 are different from those created in 1800, and again quite different from present-day work. This peculiarity of style is exploited by art historians and archaeologists to date an artefact or work of art, and in the case of archaeology, to date the archaeological site from which it was excavated. Given certain conditions this can be done with tāniko patterns also. To begin with, the article used for such purposes must be genuine and not a fake. It must have reliably established provenance and there must be other reliably established examples for comparison and checking purposes.

The style followed by a particular group such as the early Māori is closely tied in with the system of beliefs and values followed by the people. The designers of tāniko patterns created them in a definite social context for a definite clientele who understood their function and who had definite ideas about what was acceptable to their aesthetic and moral judgement. There is a conservative aspect to style, a tendency to follow the same path and not deviate too drastically from it. As is the case today, there is usually a conservative section of the population that resists and discourages change; this section is the guardian of the accepted style. But fashions change in spite of the conservatives. Change may be introduced in large doses by strong-minded pattern-makers or clients who are prepared to test public reaction and risk censure, or it may come about through very small, almost imperceptible, variations. In either event, if the innovation is not too far off from the line traditional for the moment it will become accepted by an increasing number of people until finally it is accepted by the fashionable world. The style thus moves one stage further along its developmental possibilities.

Unusual events may influence the course the style takes. The culture contact situation, for example, usually produces changes in materials and motifs. This has already been apparent in our discussion of tāniko in New Zealand.

Changes in the belief structure may also be reflected in the style; for example, when Christianity was adopted by the Māori people tattooing of the face and buttocks became identified with works of the devil and hence local tattooing styles were stifled and eventually passed out of vogue. Style associated with a particular region can also be drastically affected by warfare. It may be modified by the style of the conquerors or completely wiped out.

Style is thus very sensitive to the social state of the group. There is, however, a great deal about it that we still do not know. For example, why the Classical tāniko style has survived so long in spite of the great social changes that have occurred in Māori society is somewhat of a mystery, although I have suggested some reasons that might account for its long survival. This emphasises the highly complex nature of style dynamics. It is subject to both group and individual pressures, and to both conservative and innovative tendencies at the same time. It has to be consistent with the social and belief system but at the same time members of the society may suddenly change it for reasons difficult for an investigator to pinpoint. Though it is diagnostic of time, locality or artist, there are often examples produced that are completely baffling and quite resistant to diagnosis. Altogether, style is a many-faceted and highly interesting concept and one worthy of more attention that it receives.

As will be seen from the following analysis there are two style traditions in tāniko weaving.[2] The first I call the Pre-classic style, which ended at about 1770. The next, the Classical style tradition, was in fashion at the time of Cook's visits. Though it has undergone many changes and passed through several phases up to the present time it is still the basis of modern tāniko work and has not quite worked itself out. Under the general heading of the Classical-style tradition, I discuss the Classical style, which ends at about 1820, the Transitional style ending about 100 years later, the Early Modern Māori style ending in the late 1940s, and finally the Late Modern Māori style beginning around 1950.

The Pre-classic style tradition

This is the earliest tāniko style of which we have any evidence. In terms of fashion it was already well on the way out at the time of Cook's first visit. Fortunately for us, some examples of it were collected by Cook and Banks and are at present housed in museums in Sweden and England. They have been described by Roth and Ryden in books listed in the bibliography. It is unfortunate, however, that we do not have detailed information on when and in exactly what part of New Zealand they were collected, but we should be thankful for small mercies. Some evidence is better than none. Characteristics of the Pre-classic style tradition as exemplified by a few remaining examples are as follows:

1. The patterns, in contrast with later work, are extremely fine and intricate.
2. Compositions were either very complex, with elaborate geometrical arrangements as illustrated in plate 25 and figure 6, or they were of the type classed as the squared-meander by Roth in his 1923 publication *The Maori Mantle* (figure 7).
3. The motifs were generally picked out in single lines of white, the colour of bleached flax fibre.
4. Usually only two colours are used — black or dark brown for the background, and white for the pattern.
5. Motifs used were single oblique lines, diamonds, chevrons, scrolls and oblique, vertical and horizontal parallel lines.
6. In some patterns horizontal and vertical lines are dominant.
7. In some cases, and I suspect the cloak in plate 25 is an example, weft threads of human hair may have been used in tāniko borders.

When and for how long this particular style was in fashion is a matter for speculation but, from what we know about style, it must have been still in vogue during the early 1600s. Earlier versions of the tradition may well have been fashionable in the 1500s or even earlier. The ethnographic record merely catches the very end of its dying phase and for the rest we have no information. Some day archaeologists will find the evidence we need.

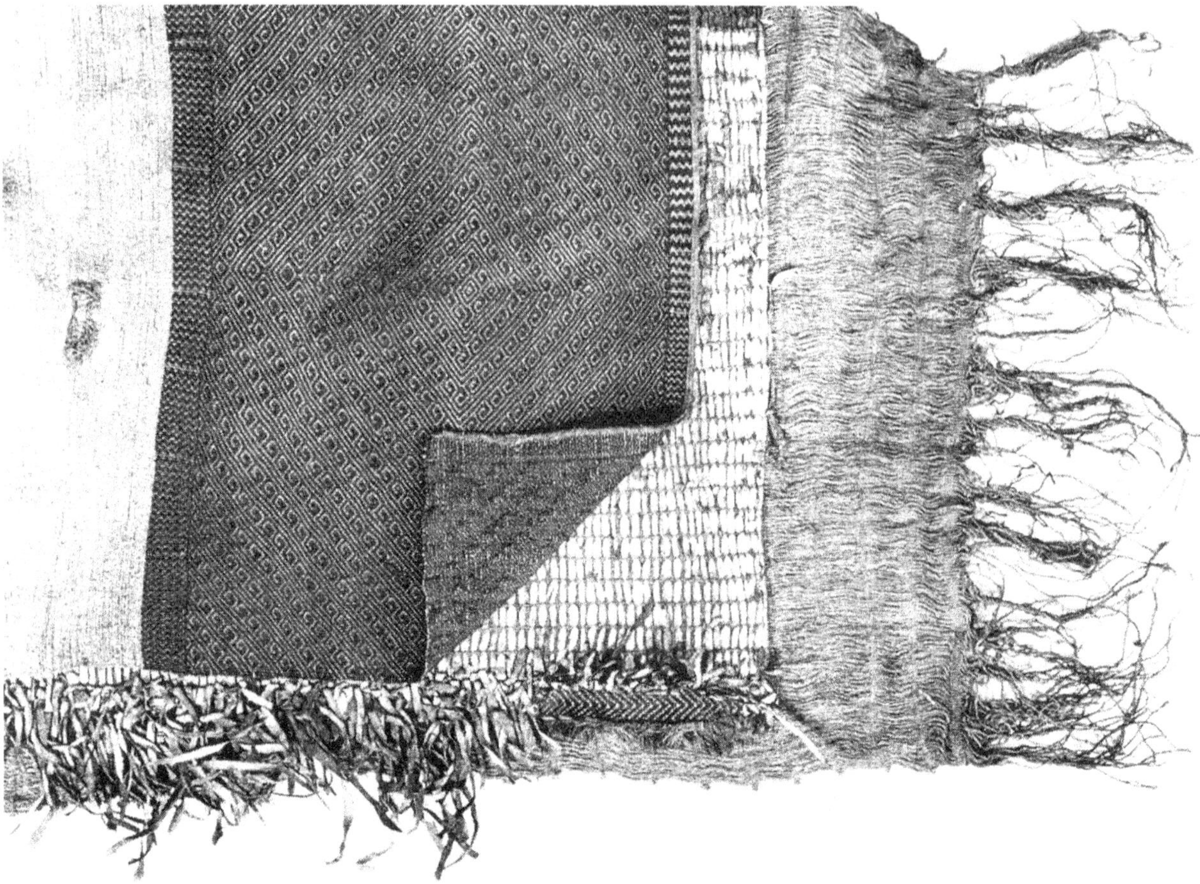

Plate 25 A fine example of the Pre-classic tāniko style. Note the use of chevrons, diamonds, scrolls and parallel lines in the highly complex composition. The cloak was collected by Banks and is now in the Ethnographic Museum of Stockholm, Sweden.

Ethnographic Museum of Stockholm

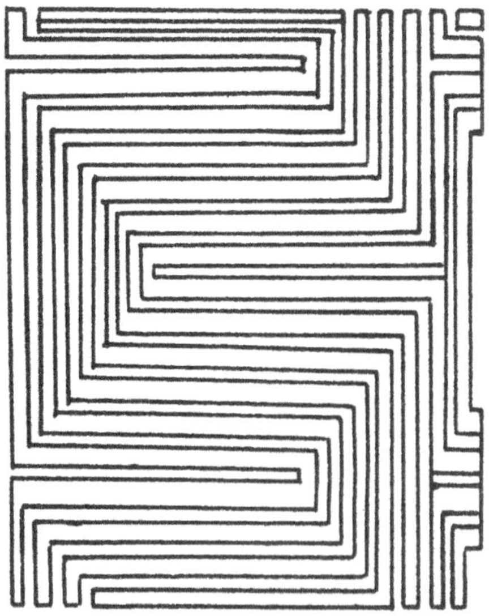

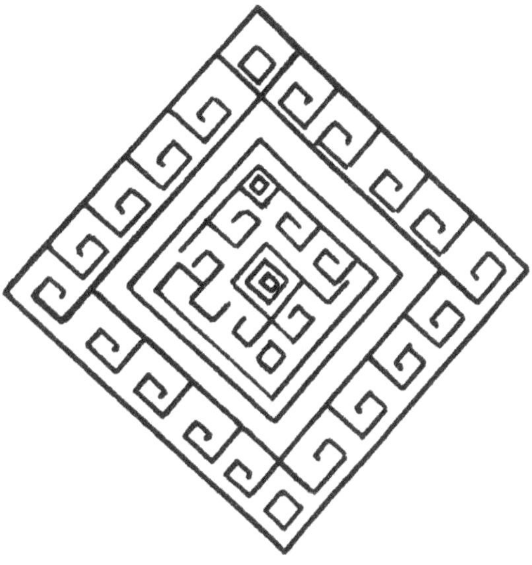

F6, F7 Examples of patterns in the Pre-classic style tradition.

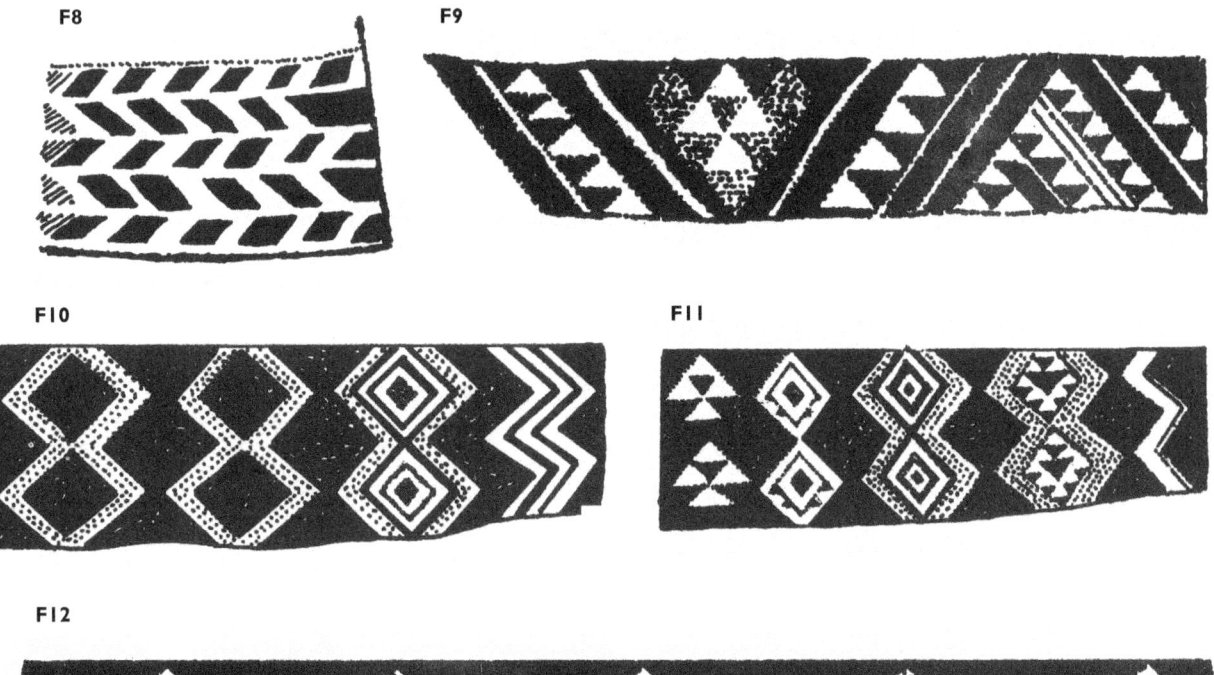

Examples of the Classical style, Phase 1.
After photographs in Hamilton

The Classical style tradition

A great many examples of this style were collected by the Cook expeditions and can be seen at the British Museum in London. It was apparently already in fashion by the middle of the eighteenth century. The Classical style represents a major break from the previous style and possess some very interesting questions as to how and why the change occurred.

Examples of the style are illustrated above. It may be argued that the reorientation was towards simplification and therefore degeneration, but I believe that this is an unkind view of Māori pattern-makers. A new style that seeks a reinterpretation of old elements necessarily has to have a beginning. Its initial phase tends to look simpler when compared with the older, fully-developed style. Given time, however, the pattern-makers soon come to grips with the new style and elaboration takes place. Examples collected by the Cook expeditions show both simple and elaborate arrangements within the Classical style and the later record does not show very complex compositions. Characteristics of the Classical style, summarily stated, are as follows:

1. More emphasis on geometric shapes as masses rather than as outlines.
2. Black forms the background to all patterns and there are large areas of it.
3. Horizontal and vertical lines, though still used, are no longer dominant and are peripheral to design arrangements.
4. Complex geometrical compositions and the squared-meander patterns are no longer used.
5. Scrolls used in the previous style pass out of vogue to reappear at a later phase.
6. Colours are restricted to various shades of red, black, white and, in isolated instances, yellow.

The Transitional style

Although the Transitional period begins in 1800 for the purposes of analysis, there is really no clear-cut break between this period and the previous one. The Classical style continues for a number of years into the Transitional period. There are, however, some clear signs of change which help to isolate the work of this period.

1. Tāniko borders become wider than the usual 12–15 centimetre lower band, and 8–10 centimetre side bands, of cloaks.
2. Patterns become more elaborate on the wider decorative band, and though black is still the background colour the tendency is to use more of it for the pattern.
3. Colours become gayer with the introduction of European wool as a weft material for tāniko borders. Purple, scarlet, green, turquoise and other non-traditional colours are used.
4. Intrusive motifs such as the Christian cross and letters of the alphabet begin to appear.
5. Warp material for cloaks and decorated borders continue to be mainly traditional.
6. There is more emphasis on geometric shapes as masses to display colour than previously.
7. Tāniko bandoliers are introduced into the costume range.

By and large, except in the matter of colour and weaving material, the Transitional style is but a continuation and elaboration of the Classical tradition. Examples from cloaks in the collection of the Auckland Institute and Museum are featured in plates 26 and 27. They are arranged typologically following a system explained in the next chapter.

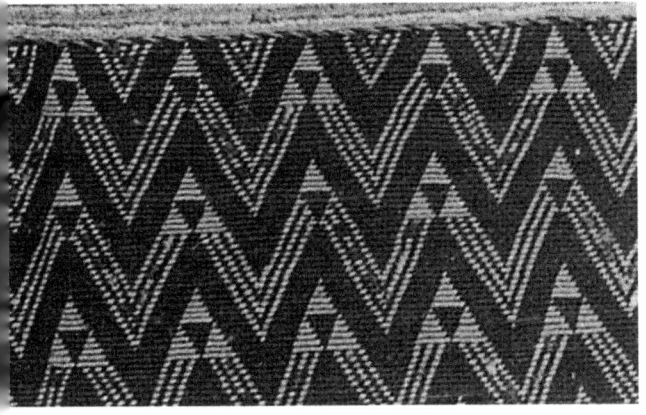

A Aramoana pattern, cloak 1497

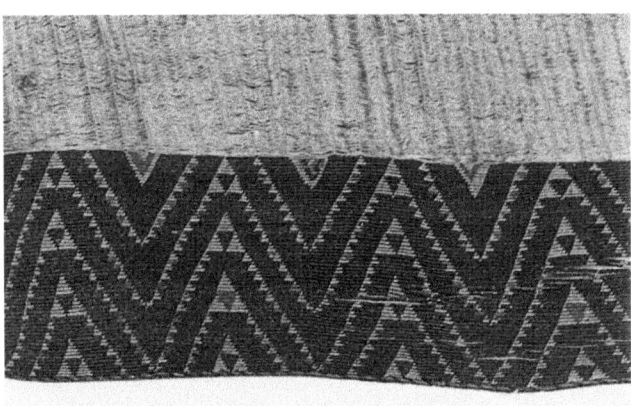

B Tukemata pattern, cloak 1500

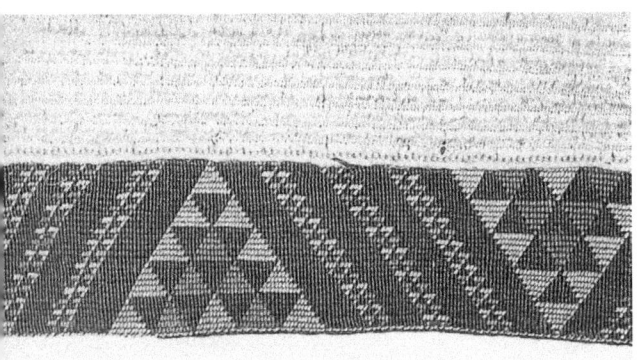

C Aonui pattern, cloak 5567E

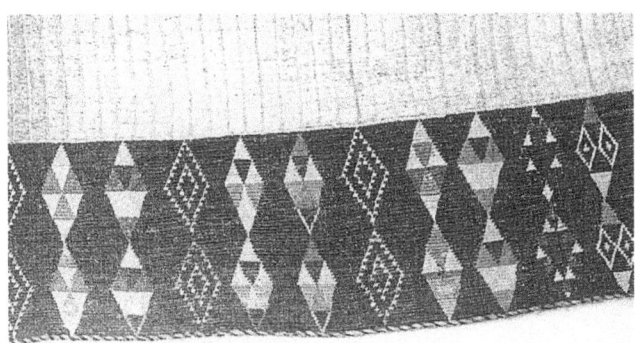

D Whakarua kōpito a waharua, cloak 815

Plates 26A–D Examples of patterns in the Transitional style from the collection of the Auckland Institute and Museum.

C.A. Schollum

Early Modern Māori style

Nominally this style begins in the 1900s, but it is essential to repeat that the date is purely arbitrary and does not represent a definite cut-off point. It ends around 1950. Important features are:

1. The introduction into the motif inventory of stars, fern leaves, houses, birds, animals and trees. Examples are graphed patterns 22 to 28 in the next chapter.
2. Such representational motifs are worked into a pattern that is based mainly on the motifs of the Classical tradition. Plate 28 illustrates the combination of new and old.
3. Belts, headbands, bodices, purses and small baskets made with the tāniko weave become numerous.

4. New Zealand symbols such as the fern leaf and kiwi together with the letters NZ become commonplace in belts and other articles made for the tourist trade.
5. The scroll is reintroduced as a motif and becomes dominant in a number of compositions. Examples are graphed patterns 19 to 21 in the next chapter.
6. Macramé twine and fishing lines become popular as warp materials, and coloured silks as wefts.
7. There is a resurgence of tāniko weaving during this period but by the fourth decade it is again on the decline.

The resurgence of tāniko weaving coincides with the general movement towards resuscitating Māori art and craft activities during the late thirties. It was felt that this was good for the Māori spirit and morale. The Māori education system did much to encourage the survival of tāniko weaving. The style period closes with weavers divided into two camps: the 'free-for-all' weavers who are very modern in the motifs they use; and the conservative weavers who shun the newfangled motifs as much as possible. An example of work done by the latter is featured in plate 29.

Late Modern Māori style

Beginning at about 1950 this style, like the previous one, is no longer consistent throughout Māori society. Style has become fragmented and specialised; the weavers being divided into several divisions that cater to different social and ceremonial needs. This period could well be the crossroads for the Classical style tradition. It may continue into another phase or it may die out, giving way to a new orientation that future pattern-makers will follow.

The general characteristics listed here are based mainly on the work of non-traditional weavers whose work on a quantitative count would outnumber that of the traditionalists. Best quality work, however, tends to be produced by the conservatives.

1. The rejection of the tāniko technique after nearly 200 years of Western contact, for all but the most highly valued articles.
2. Its replacement by tapestry weaving.
3. The reintroduction of wool as weft material because this is best suited to work on a tapestry mesh.
4. A general tendency towards more traditionally based pattern motifs for articles such as headbands, bodices and bandoliers. This is due to the modern practice of judging dance performances and allocating marks for costume.
5. Some weavers continue to incorporate new representational motifs, for example, Auckland's harbour bridge has been captured in tāniko by one Auckland weaver.
6. A tendency to restrict colours to the range of the Classical style.

This period is full of anomalies. The conservatives try to work in the style of the Transitional and Classical periods while the modems exploit new possibilities. In between these two extremes are many competent weavers who follow a middle-of-the-road policy. The conservatives tend to produce for high ceremonial such as the tangi, inter-tribal gatherings, regal, vice-regal and ministerial ceremonials where tribal honour is at stake. Though tribal honour is still a consideration for the non-conservatives, much more latitude is allowed them in outfitting dancing teams in costume. Some of the latter produce work for the tourist. More innovative weavers produce mixed media work for art galleries and exhibitions. Plate 1 illustrates rather well the tāniko work of the Late Modern Māori style.

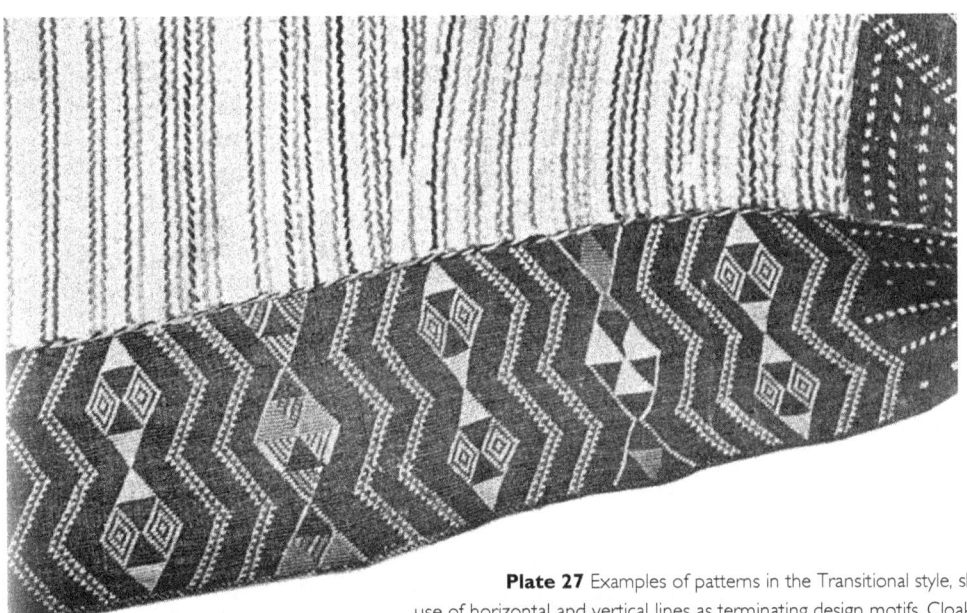

Plate 27 Examples of patterns in the Transitional style, showing the use of horizontal and vertical lines as terminating design motifs. Cloaks from the Auckland Institute and Museum. Above, an example of the use of horizontal and vertical lines in the Transitional period. Rau kiimara pattern, cloak 5565. Below, horizontal bars used as a terminating device in a pattern sequence. Rau kiimara pattern, cloak from Grey Collection.

C.A. Schollum

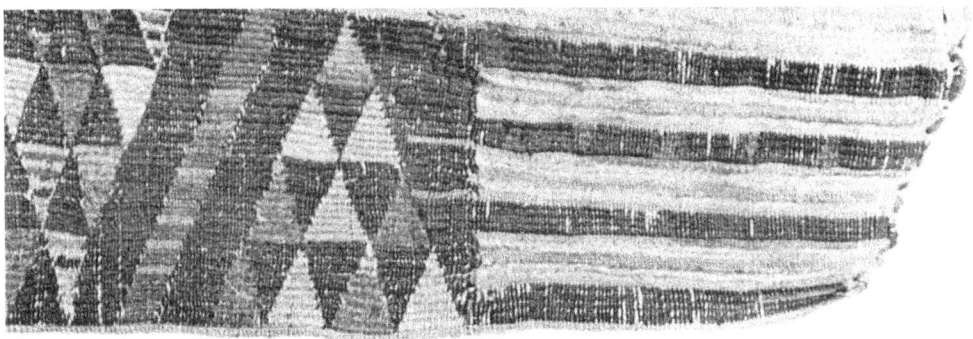

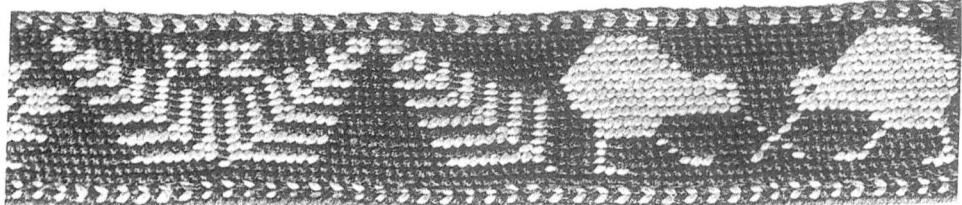

Plate 28 A tāniko belt 97 centimetres long and just over 25 centimetres wide illustrates the freestyle of the Early Modern Māori period. Colours used are gold and black. The belt belongs to Mrs Joy Biggs, Auckland.
C.A. Schollum

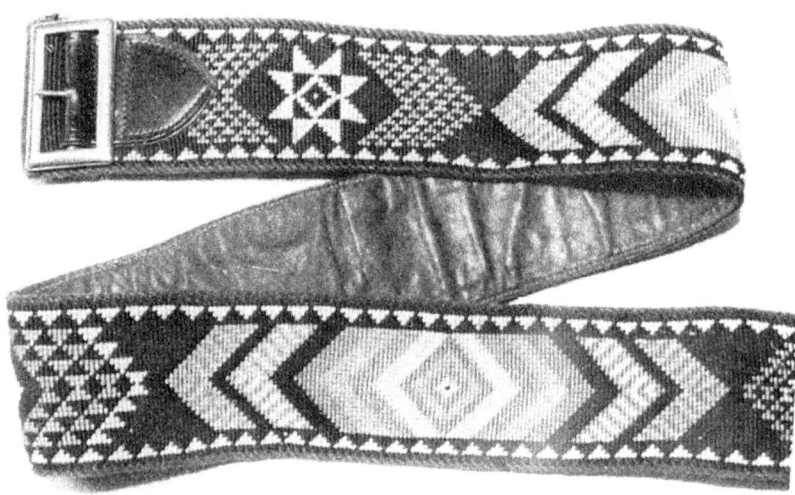

Plate 29 A beautifully finished belt made in the Early Modern Māori style by a more conservative weaver. It is 122 centimetres long and 5 centimetres wide. Colours used are black, red, gold, blue and white. It belongs to Mrs Joy Biggs.
G.A. McCracken

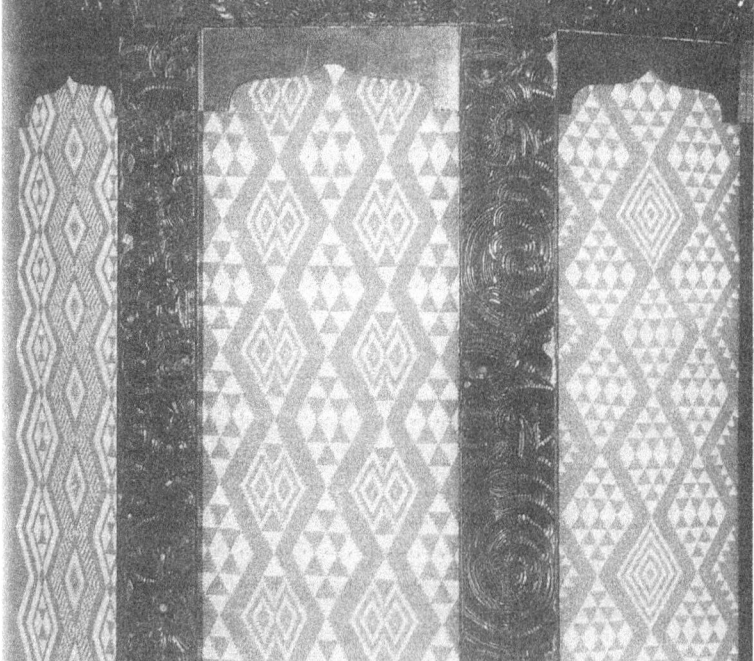

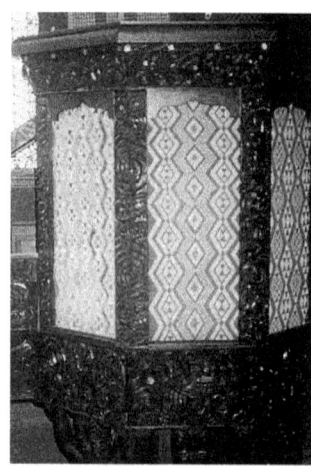

Plate 30 & detail Tāniko applied to a pulpit at the Tikitiki church, made by Mrs Dick George of Waiomatatini following the traditional methods of preparing the strands. At left, detail of tāniko panels at the Tikitiki church.
Len Hetet

Style and ritual

One of the strongest forces in primitive society that acts to preserve the purity and continuity of a style is the ritual that weavers have to undergo at initiation and thereafter observe.

At the baptism ceremony known as tohi a Māori female child was publicly dedicated to the pursuits of adult and responsible women. Spells were cast at the umbilical cord through which they were supposed to enter the child's stomach. As the girl grew up she observed over the years the weaving activities of her household and assisted where she could. From near the age of puberty onwards she was watched carefully by the older women for signs of a natural flair for weaving. The tactics adopted were to discourage the girl from taking up weaving seriously; she would be sent out to play with the children or told she was a dunce. No one would bother to teach her any new technique until she demonstrated a very strong desire to learn. By this time she would have put in many hours of practise to prove her determination. A few more years of practise would follow, during which time she would acquire the necessary techniques to reproduce patterns used by her mother or grandmother and other close female relatives.

She would as a matter of course learn the rules and superstitions of the weaving craft. She would, for example, learn that fine garments should be woven only during the daytime. At sunset the sacred peg must be taken down and the weaving rolled up and put away. Weaving must be done under cover and at the approach of strangers must be hidden from sight. If a weft thread is too short, the weaver will become widowed. If the weaving peg falls over, a visitor is coming and so work must cease, and so on.

When the novice felt secure enough to establish herself as a fully fledged weaver the priest was approached to perform the ritual. On the appointed day a hut or house called the wharepara was made sacred for the purpose and into this the priest and novice went. The novice sat on a mat with two weaving pegs before her, the left one plain and the sacred peg on the right carved. A thread was stretched across the pegs to accommodate the warp threads that were folded over it. Now the priest recited spells aimed at helping the novice to complete quickly the pattern piece she was to weave. At the completion of the spell the novice bent over the sacred peg and bit the top of it, which was usually carved in the form of a head. The spell entered her mouth through the peg and finally lodged in her stomach. She then took up the two-pair interlocking weft, called here the aha tapu (sacred thread) and began the pattern piece. Apparently neither she nor the priest could leave the house until this was completed, hence the concern for speed in weaving.

In the next ceremony, after the completion of the pattern piece, more spells were recited. It was called hurihanga takapau (turning the floor mat). The initiate bit or ate a piece of sour thistle and the spell is designed to force home the sacred knowledge and make it permanent were cast. After this the weaver was free to rejoin her community, but this time as a recognised adult weaver who would play her part in keeping and following the regional style.[3]

The ritual ceremonies, rules and beliefs play a vital part in bringing pressure to bear on weavers to reproduce and create 'properly' within the village style. In small communities there is little room for the reactionary. There is a correct way of performing every task, from cutting the flax leaves to weaving the pattern. It is also evident that the beliefs are directed at technical competence and upon the preservation of style from the prying eyes of strangers. Hence ritual is a powerful agent in maintaining constancy and stability of style.

Conclusion

The stylistic analysis of tāniko brings out very strikingly the changes that have occurred in this art form. It is interesting that when certain motifs pass out of fashion they do not necessarily remain dead; when they reappear, however, they do not necessarily follow the original form.

This is brought out in the case of the scroll motif first used in the Pre-classical style and illustrated in plate 25. During that period it was a minor motif, but when it reappears in the Early Modern Māori style it becomes a major motif in a series of patterns.

The last phase of the Classical style tradition may well indicate what happens to style in its last stages of development. In its earlier phases it forms a kind of national or all-pervading style followed by most, if not all, of the community. Then it splits into high and low divisions of the style, and a struggle takes place between those who would retain the purity of traditionalism and those who would introduce innovations. But I suspect that a time comes when the addition of modifications to the general style reaches a saturation point. After this there is little aesthetic pleasure to be gained by such minor changes and a major reinterpretation has to be made. It is probably at this point that the great artist emerges, whose work is fully appreciated by posterity and roundly condemned by his contemporaries!

Notes
1. Schapiro, 1 953, p. 287.
2 By a style tradition I mean a style that, though constantly changing through time and space, nevertheless retains its basic characteristics.
3 The information is based on Best, 1898, p. 628.

6

The Classification of Tāniko Patterns

Whereas style was not discussed in detail by earlier students of tāniko, the same cannot be said of classification, as a brief review of the literature will confirm. The earliest classification was advanced by Buck in 1911. Using motifs as the basic criterion of grouping, he suggested there were three main types of tāniko patterns:

1. Triangle-based patterns, in which the main motifs are large triangles with bases alternating. Such patterns are called aronui (broad aspect).
2. Chevron-based patterns. There are two types within this category: plain zigzags in red, white or yellow, against a black background, called aramoana (ocean path); and serrated or toothed zigzags, called tukemata (eyebrow). The serrations are termed niho (teeth).
3. Diamond based patterns called whakarua kōpito (to make two points).[1]

Buck's classification system remained unchallenged for nearly 50 years. His pioneer effort still forms the main basis of all subsequent classifications and provides a starting point for any discussion of the subject. He was also concerned with evolutionary theory, that is, with trying to determine which motifs came first along a development sequence. He postulated, for example, that triangle motifs were older than continuous chevrons because they were universal throughout New Zealand. Later studies fail to confirm or to refute this theory. Both these motifs were employed in the Pre-classic style and both continue to be used today. Which came before the other, therefore, remains a matter for speculation.

In 1960 Phillipps restated Buck's classification as follows:

1. Aramoana. Patterns based on plain zigzags.
2. Tukemata. Patterns based on serrated zigzags.
3. Aonui. Patterns based on triangles.
4. Whakarua kōpito. Patterns based on diamonds.

Up to this point in his classification the system follows Buck except that the order is different and the term aonui has been changed from aronui. Phillipps was the first student since Buck to draw attention to a serious omission in the early system. He realised that Buck had failed to account for patterns featuring horizontal lines, or 'oblongs' as he preferred to call them. To close the gap he suggested a fifth class of motifs should be added, namely patterns in which the oblong motif was used.

Our stylistic analysis in the previous chapter confirms that Phillipps was correct in doing this, but by limiting the class to oblongs he lessened its value, for both horizontal and vertical lines were used in tāniko patterns as far back as the Pre-classic style, and usually together. These motifs contrast with the predominance of oblique lines in patterns of the Classical style. Into Phillipps' fifth class, then, I would include horizontal and vertical line motifs and this would account for a number of patterns that would otherwise be excluded by his classification system.

It is perhaps needless to emphasise that a good classification system should categorise the greatest number of items being classified. Ideally, it should account for all cases. The addition of a fifth class certainly helps to take in a few more patterns from the 'leftover' heap, but as we shall see later there are still more to be dealt with.

Phillipps also undertook a comprehensive analysis of triangle and diamond patterns used in tāniko, exploring variations of motif and colour combinations used by the pattern-makers. This analysis is also a valuable contribution to the study of tāniko.[2]

Terence Barrow, another student who has studied tāniko, also employed Buck's classification system and terminology in an article published in 1962.

In my own case, it is perhaps a sad commentary on the state of my knowledge at the time that in the earlier edition of this work neither style nor classification was discussed. As an art teacher my main concern then was in teaching tāniko as a craft and in creating new tāniko patterns still in the spirit of the old. To digress for a moment, it is characteristic of the writers mentioned here that they have all worked within different frameworks. Buck's evolutionary interest has already been mentioned. Phillipps, though he devoted time to pattern analysis, was mainly interested in describing and classifying patterns. Barrow was interested primarily in the social function of Māori cloaks, and tāniko tended to be peripheral to this concern. My own interests have changed radically, from those of an unsophisticated young art teacher to the wider framework of anthropology.

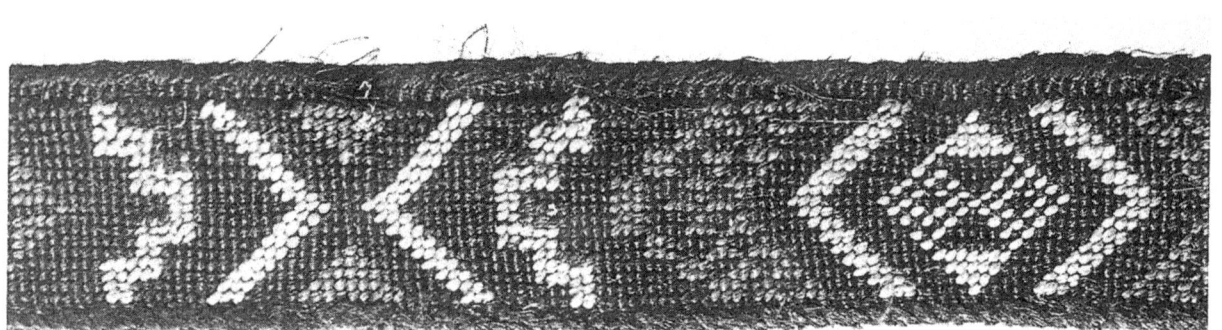

Plate 31 In black, gold and brown, this belt, made by Mrs June Tere of Te Kuiti in 1955, is remarkable for the fact that it is made of traditionally prepared and dyed fibres. It is called a muka (flax fibre) belt to distinguish it from others made in macramé twine and coloured silks. This article is in the collection of Mrs Joy Biggs, Auckland. C.A. Schollum

Another fault with some of the earlier classifications is that the writers did not always make clear what they were doing, and what basic assumptions they were using. The fact that an adequate classification system should aim at being exhaustive was either not realised at all or, if it was, it was never stated. Furthermore, while it is obvious that Buck was using motifs as the main criterion of classification, he did not say so; nor did he explain why he chose motifs and not something else. As it turns out, however, he was using a folk classification system, but it took many years for me to recognise this simple fact. It was not until I had the good fortune to interview a very sharp and knowledgeable Ngāti Pikiao informant at Te Teko that I realised that weavers themselves classify and name patterns according to the dominant motif used and that this was the system adopted by Buck. This system is consistent also with what we have discovered to be the most persistent aspect of tāniko generally, namely, the motifs themselves. Perhaps folk classifications exhibit consistencies that would not be present in an arbitrarily devised system. In any case, the unstated premises and information we have now brought forward throw an entirely different light on the Buck system, and help us to understand how it works and why it has persisted.

Another fault of previous classifiers is that they did not provide enough illustrative material to exemplify the various types set up.

In proposing yet another system I hope to remedy some of these shortcomings. As I am following and extending Buck's system there is no need to repeat the justification of it. My own does aim at exhaustiveness. It focuses attention on the dominant motif used and discounts material and technique of manufacture, which we have found to be not fundamental to tāniko. The time element is also ignored in the present discussion because this has been dealt within the previous chapter.

The present system takes into account much material that was not available to Buck in 1911, nor in 1926 when his major work was published. For example, evidence for the Pre-classic style did not become convincing until the publication in 1963 of the Banks Collection in Stockholm, and of course Buck had no way of forecasting developments in the Modern period.

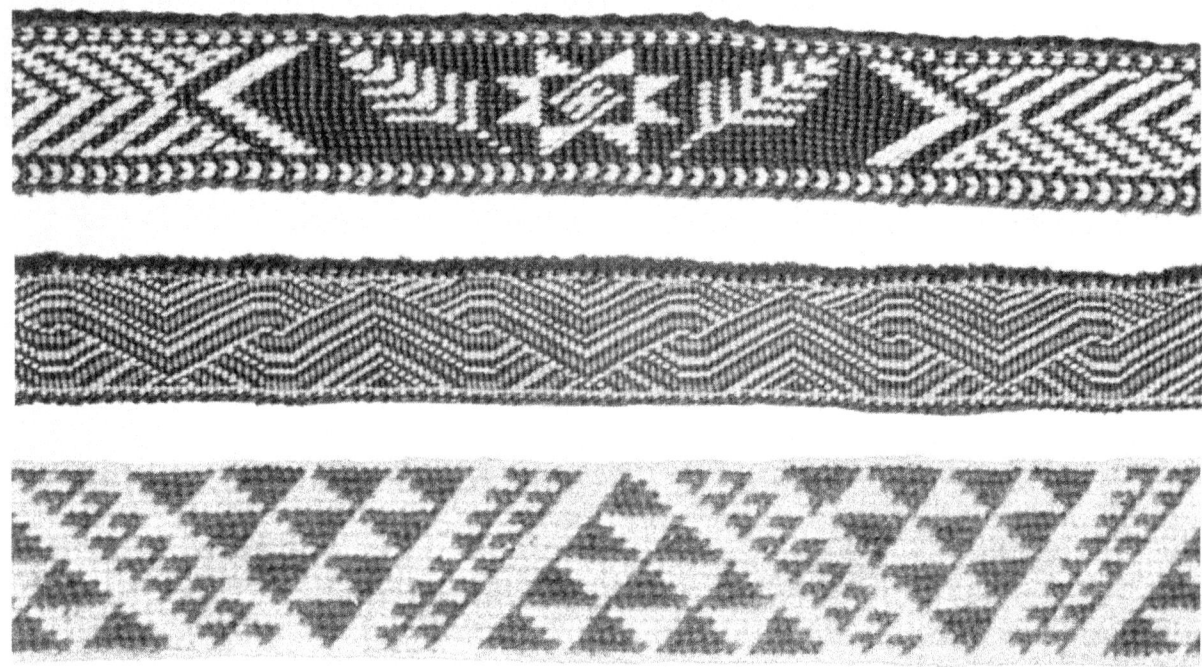

Plate 32 Three completed belts of the Modern period. The top belt was made for the author by Mrs Anne Whaipooti of Ruatoria. The middle one, an exceptionally fine piece, was made by Mr W. Hohepa of Waima, Northland, and is now owned by Mrs Dick George of Waiomatatini. The lower belt was made by an unknown Waikato weaver and belongs to the photographer's father.
C.A. McCracken

Patterns used as illustrative material here have been graphed so as to be in the form of greatest use to practical weavers. Photographic examples of woven material are scattered throughout the book and some of these have been arranged typologically in chapter five. By using so many examples of each type it is hoped to accomplish two aims: first, to help in understanding the system, and second, to provide practical weavers with a host of pattern possibilities from which they can choose.

A classification system for tāniko patterns

Class 1 Aramoana and Tukemata patterns. These are patterns or parts of pattern sequences in which the dominant motif is the chevron. There are two varieties in Class 1: aramoana or plain chevrons are exemplified by graphed patterns 1 to 3, and in plate 26A; the tukemata or serrated variety is exemplified in plate 26B.

Class 2 Aronui or Aonui patterns. The dominant motif used in this class is the triangle, plain or embellished, and with the bases alternating.
Examples are given in graphed patterns 4 to 9 and in plate 26C.

Class 3 Patikitiki patterns. These are patterns in which the dominant motif is the single diamond. Examples are graphed patterns 10 to 14. The class name is taken from pattern 13, another version of which is illustrated in plate 33.

Class 4 Waharua (two mouths or openings) or whakarua kōpito (two points). In this class two or more diamond motifs are placed one above the other as in plate 260. Graphed pattern 15 is yet to be extended downwards to exemplify fully this type. Pattern 16 is another example.

Class 5 Patterns based on horizontal and vertical lines. This class takes in the squared-meander type of the Pre-classic era as well as patterns 17 and 18. Further examples are shown in plates 27 and 34.

Class 6 Patterns based on the scroll. Patterns in which the scroll is dominant belong to this class. Examples are graphed patterns 19 to 21 and the centre belt in plate 32.

Class 7 Patterns based on representational motifs. This includes all motifs that are obviously representational, such as trees and the harbour bridge of Auckland, and also includes all non-traditional motifs such as crosses, letters of the alphabet, circles and so on. Examples are graphed patterns 22 to 28, the top belt in plate 32, and the belt in plate 28.

Viewing patterns

A note should be added here concerning the way tāniko patterns are viewed by an observer.

In some patterns there are two aspects — a positive and a negative — both of which are attractive. The positive pattern arrangement is traced out in colour and is the first aspect, and often the only one, which an observer notices. The negative pattern is seen in terms of background and one must make a conscious effort to see it.

A difficulty of viewpoint arises in the graphed patterns, in which areas of light and shade have been reversed as in a negative film. The consequence of such reversal is that an observer sees the negative aspect of the pattern very easily and often this is mistaken for the positive pattern.

As an example of what is meant here, examine patterns 4 to 7. In all of these, the negative aspect in white comes forward into consciousness while black recedes into the background. When these patterns are actually translated into woven material the white squares become the black background and the black squares become areas of colour, so that it is the positive aspect of the design which clamours for attention.

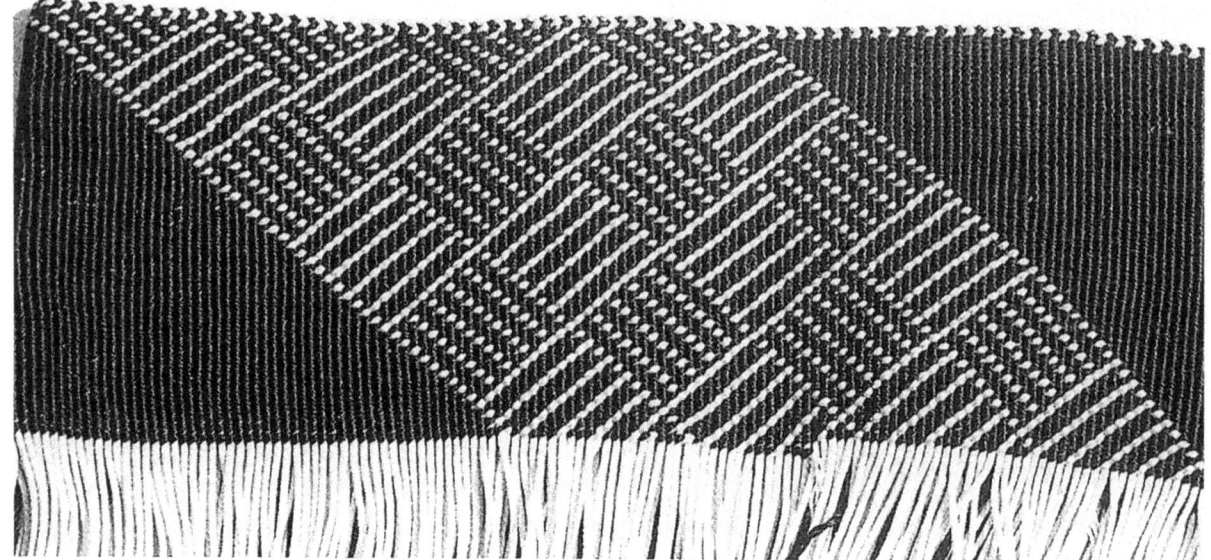

Plate 33 This unfinished purse, made by Mrs Dick George of Waiomatatini, illustrates a modern application of tāniko and the very difficult technique of weaving in continuous circles to avoid an unsightly join on one side of the object. The weaver prefers the fine line of the Pre-classic style.
G.A. McCracken

The naming of patterns

In his book on primitive art Adam said: 'The connection between the pattern and its symbolic meaning arises in two ways: either by deliberate simplification of a representational design as in North-west America, or else by the observation of incidental resemblances between geometric pattern and its naturalistic interpretation.'[3] The latter seems to fit the Māori case fairly well .The pātikitiki-papaki-rango (graphed pattern 13) was so named because the central motif looked somewhat like the diamond-shaped fly-swatter made of plaited flax that was attached to a wooden handle. The name aramoana (ocean path), a little more picturesque, was labelled so presumably because continuous chevrons looked like stylised waves. I know of no case in tāniko where one can claim with confidence that an abstract motif was a deliberate simplification of some representational design.

It would appear that the labels attached to patterns by the Māori were of no great importance to students interested in tracing the derivation of abstract motifs. Each tribe had its own list of pattern names, which, along with the patterns themselves, weavers attempted to keep secret.

Boas makes clear that among the Californian Indians names for the same design motif also varied from tribe to tribe,[4] so that the New Zealand Māori is apparently not alone in this respect. An obvious function of pattern names was to enable weavers to communicate easily with other members of the group about the designs they used.

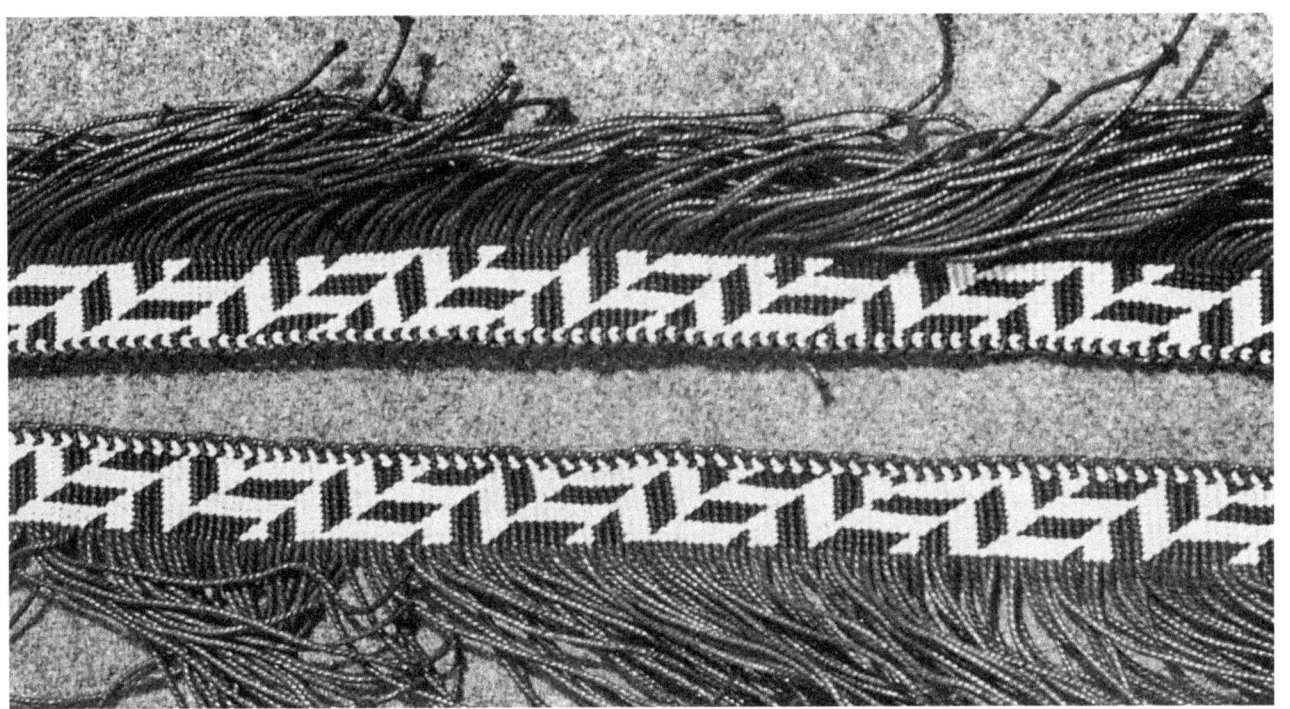

Plate 34 In this belt made by Mrs June Mead, formerly of Ruatoria, casting on and the weaving of the pattern (graphed pattern 17) have been completed. The casting-off stage, still to be done, folds the warp ends behind the belt, from which position they can be cut. The completed article is now in the possession of Mr J. Bishop of Whatawhata, Waikato.

G.A. McCracken

Non-weaving applications of tāniko

Among the carvers of Mataatua tāniko patterns provide a shared pool of images for decorated meeting houses. In the meeting house Mataatua recently returned to Whakatane from the Otago Museum, tāniko patterns appear above every tukutuku panel. These patterns are painted on and are often complex compositions. Other houses in Mataatua share this feature, for example, Ruataupare at Te Teko. Mataatua was built in 1875 so this feature is over a hundred years old.

Recently tāniko patterns were painted in the porch of Te Herenga Waka, the carved house opened in 1986 at Victoria University, Wellington. The carver responsible for the decorative plan of this house was Clarence Takirirangi Smith and he was assisted by Nick Tupara who played a key role in the painted patterns of the house.

Notes
1. From Buck's article 'On the Maori Art of Weaving Cloaks, Capes and Kilts'.
2. Phillipps, in his *Maori Rafter and Taniko Designs*.
3. Adam, 1940, p. 28.
4. Boas, 1955, pp. 110–11.

Graphed Patterns

Class 1 Aramoana and tukemata patterns in which the chevron motif is dominant.

1 Two-colour pattern, 10 weft lines.

2 Three-colour pattern, 30 weft lines. May be reversed to form a class 3 pattern and further extended to a class 4 pattern.

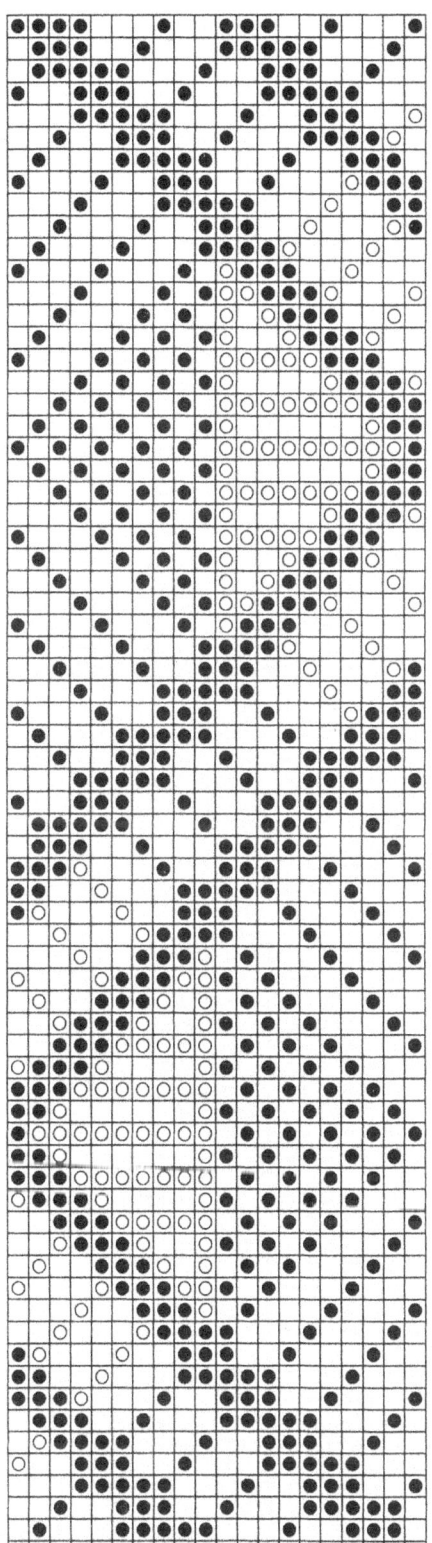

3 Three-colour pattern, 20 weft lines. Can be reversed to form a diamond pattern of 44 wefts.

Class 2 Aronui and aonui patterns in which the triangle is the dominant motif.

4 Two colours, 10 weft lines. This pattern is called taupokipoki (turn over).

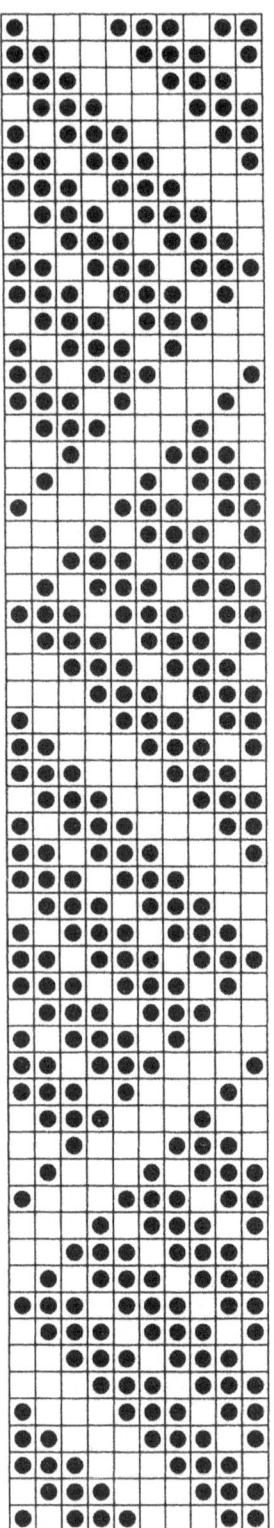

5 Two colours, 10 weft lines. May be continued downwards to form diamonds, will then become a 20-weft pattern.

6 Two colours. 16 weft lines. A third colour can be introduced into the triangles. The triangle is flanked by teeth (niho) forming a series called whakaniho (to form teeth).

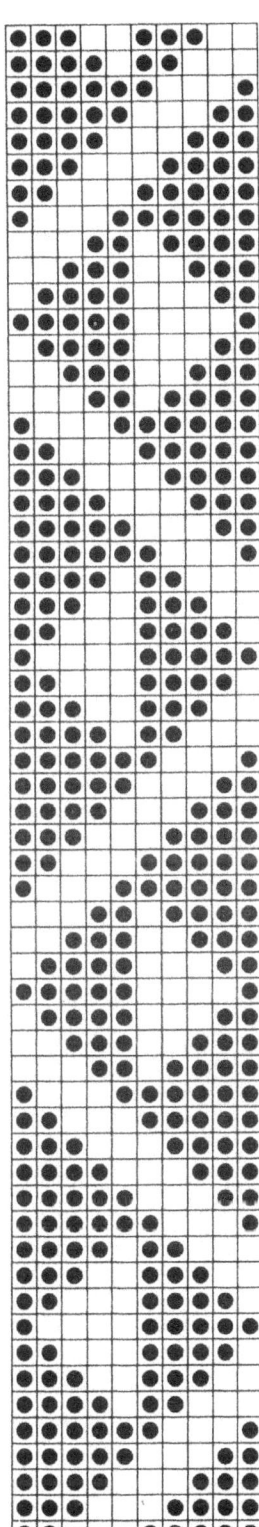

7 Two colours, 10 weft lines.

8 Two or three colours, 16 weft lines. May be extended to form a 32-weft pattern.

9 Three or four colours, 29 weft rows. May be reversed and extended to a class 3 pattern of 57 weft lines.

10 Two or three colours, 19 weft lines. May be continued to form a class 4 pattern of 37 weft lines.

Class 3 Patikitiki patterns in which the single diamond is the dominant motif.

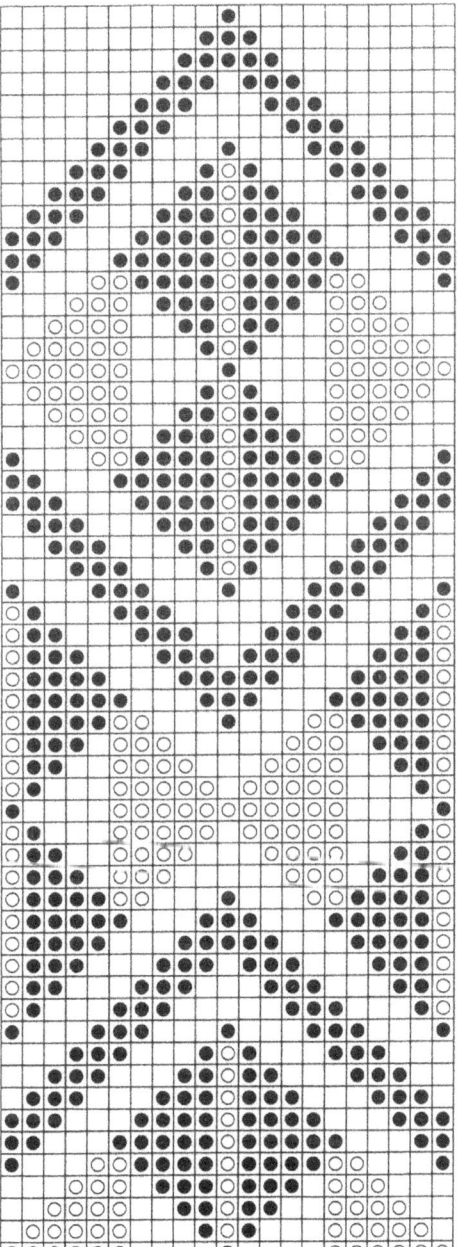

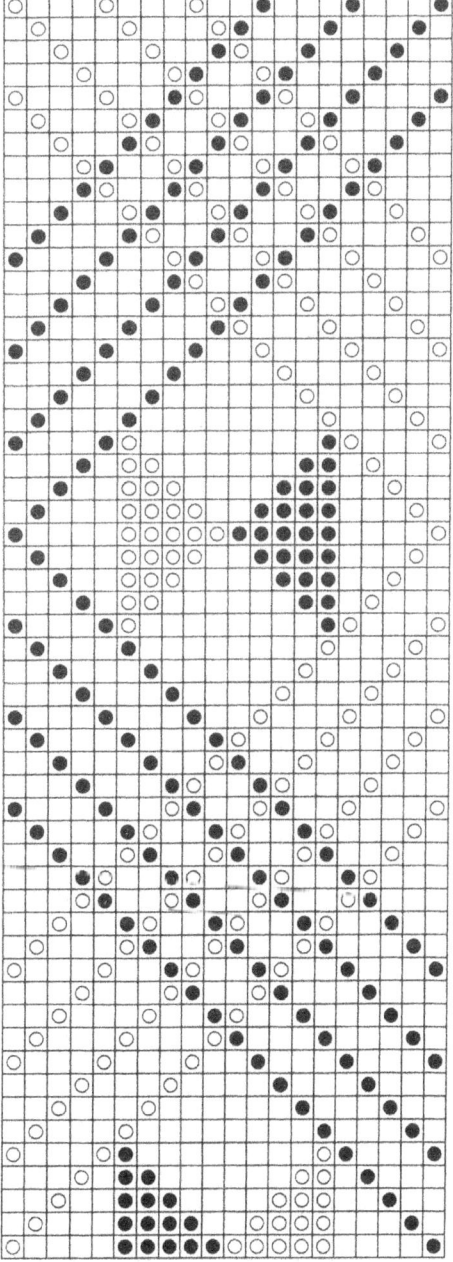

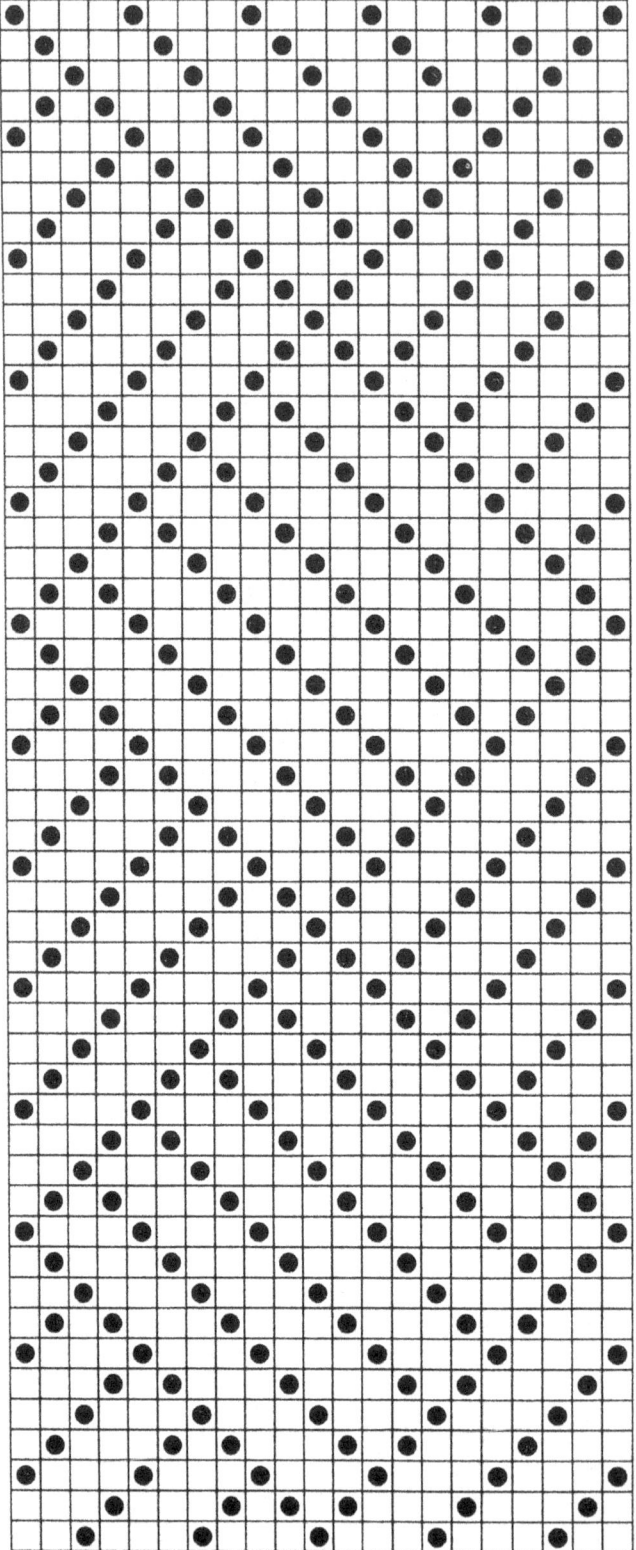

13 Two colours, 21 weft rows. This is the pātikitiki-papaki-rango favoured by East Coast weavers. The pattern takes its name from a flax fan used to keep flies away from a corpse.

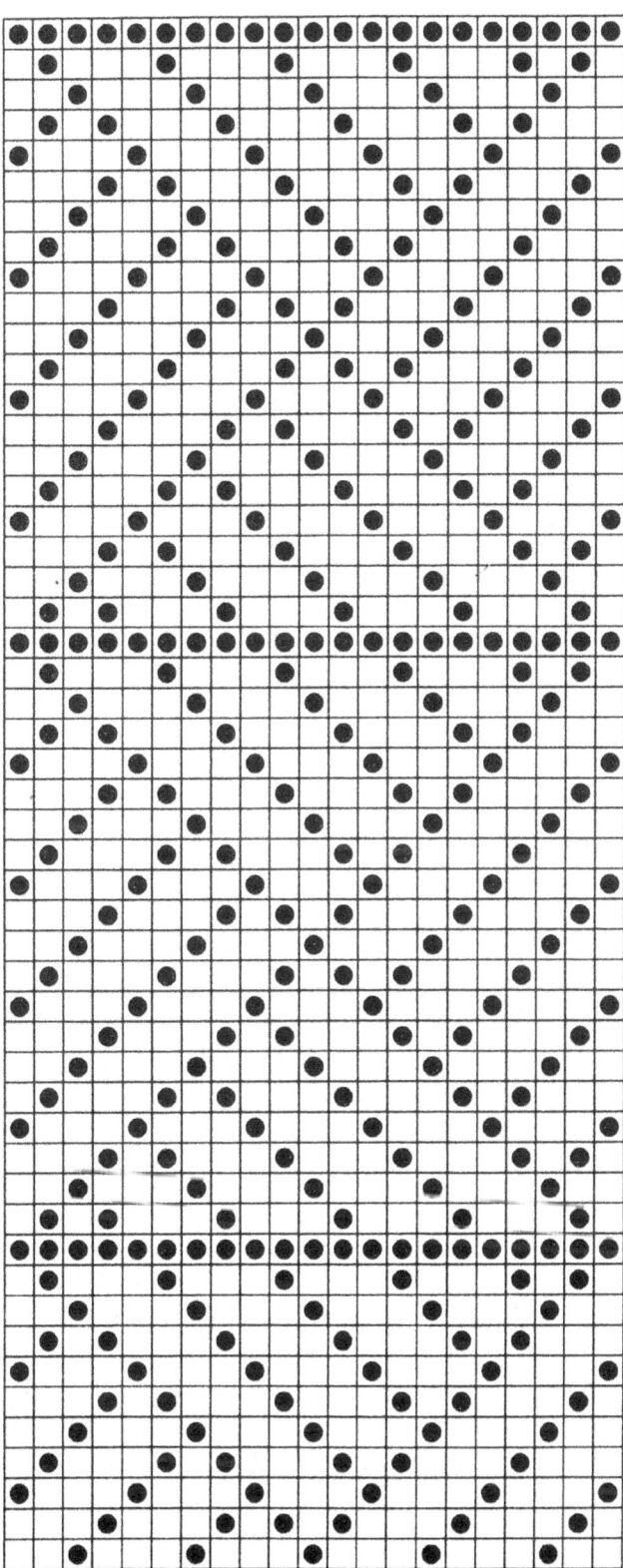

14 Two colours, 21 wefts. This pattern is called pāpaka (crab).

Class 4 Waharua (two mouths) or whakarua kōpito (two points) patterns, which are based on more than one diamond placed one above the other.

15 Two, three or four colours, 40 weft rows. The pattern needs to be extended downward to 79 weft rows to be fully representative of the class. Also the motifs need to be spaced out by as many as 30 extra warp lines.

16 Three or four colours, 57 weft rows deep and 70 warps wide. The pattern may be extended downwards in units of 14 wefts, and it should be opened out considerably by 20 to 30 warps to gets its full effect. Like the previous pattern, it has been constricted in order to fit the page.

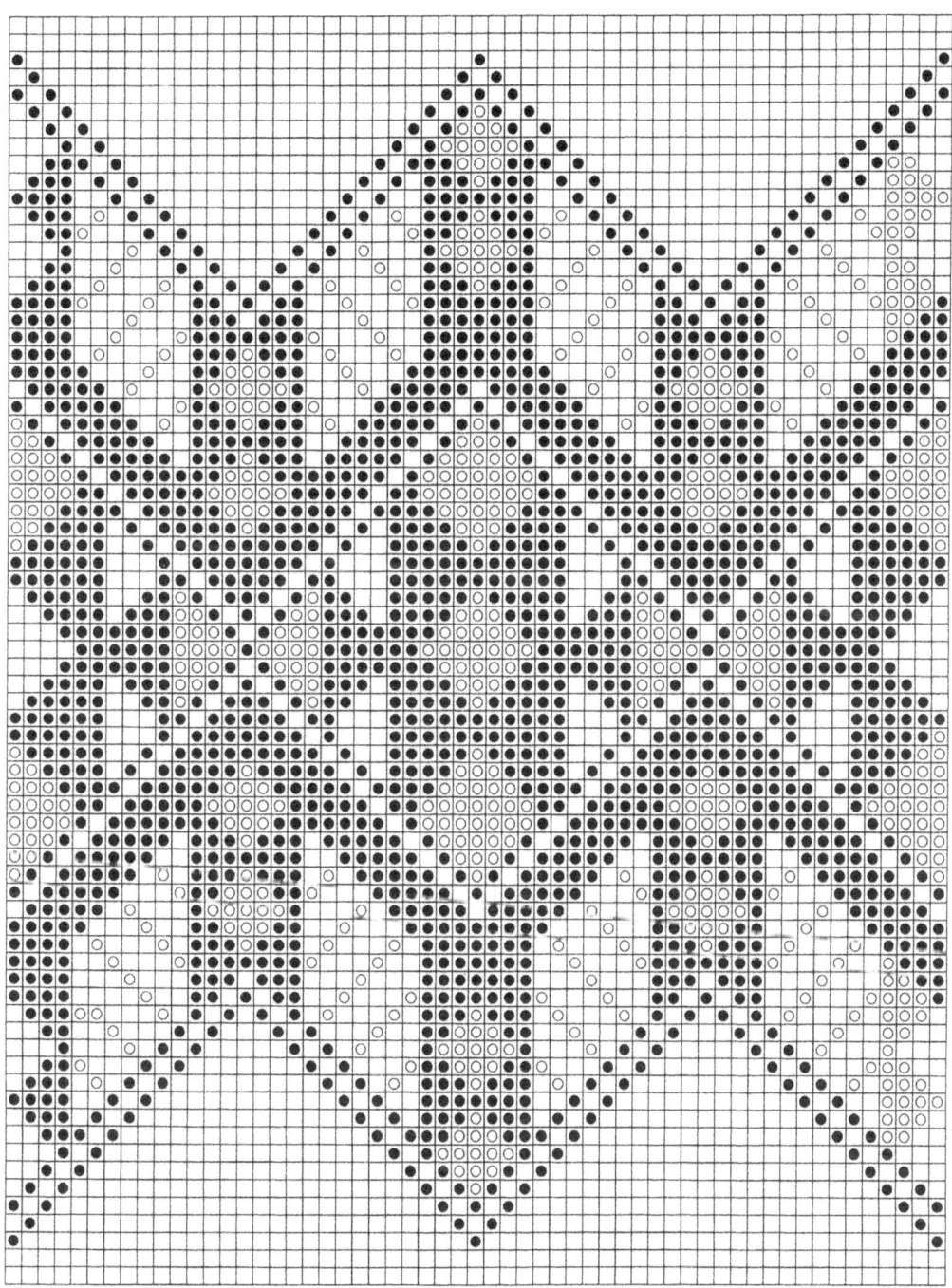

Class 5 Patterns based on horizontal and vertical lines. The type may be called raukūmara (sweet-potato leaves) after the patterns illustrated in plates 27 and 34.

17 Two or three colours, 18 weft rows. This particular pattern is called tawatawa (mackerel) by East Coast weavers.

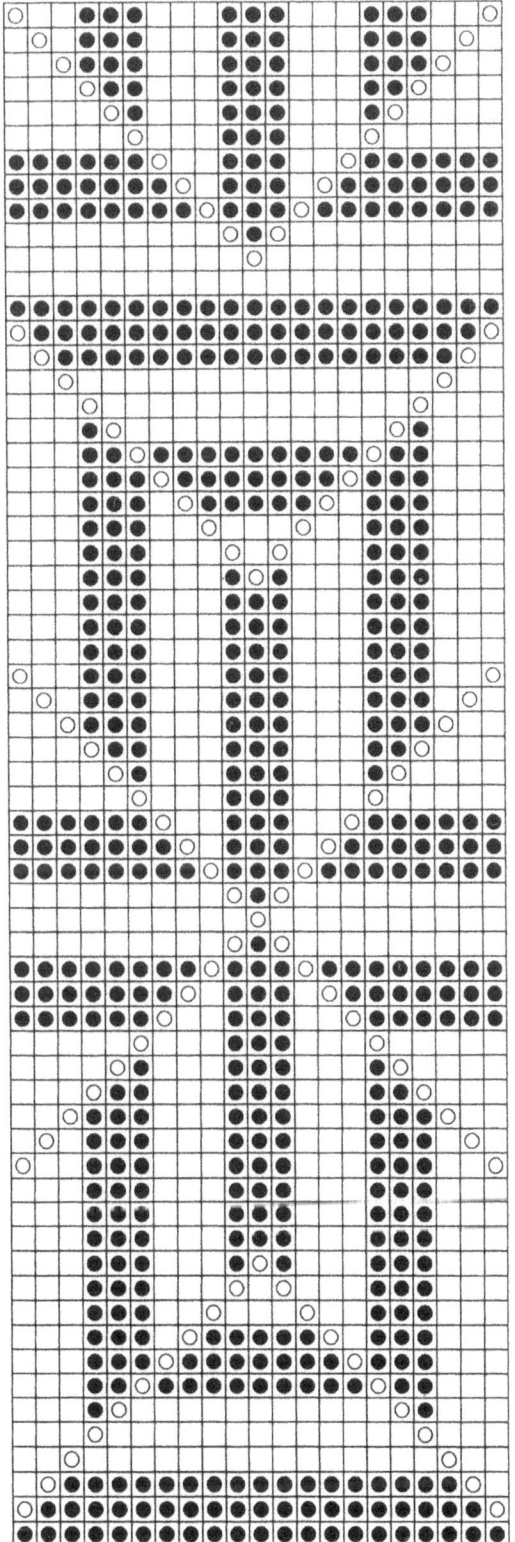

18 Three colours, 21 weft lines. This pattern is called kaokao (armpit) because of the up-ended chevrons running through it.

Class 6 Patterns based on the scroll. These may be called kōwhaiwhai patterns since they are obviously based on rafter patterns used in meeting houses.

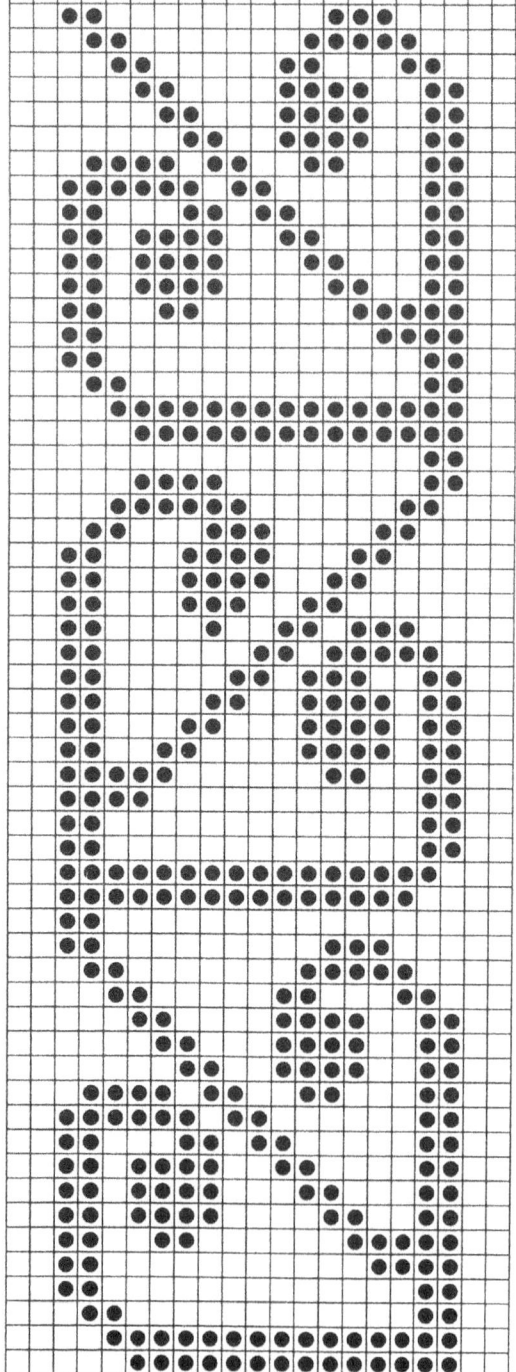

19 Two colours, 15 weft lines.

20 Two colours, 17 wefts.

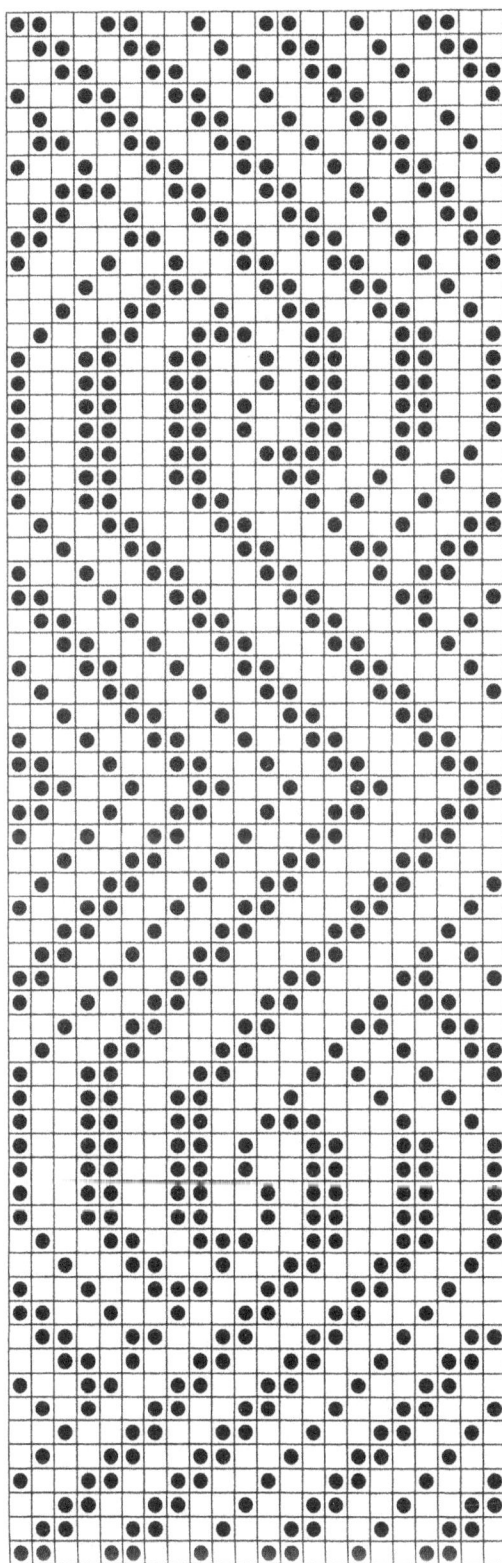

21 Two or three colours, 22 wefts.

Class 7 Patterns based on representational motifs. The motifs illustrated here form a minor theme in pattern compositions based on other types.

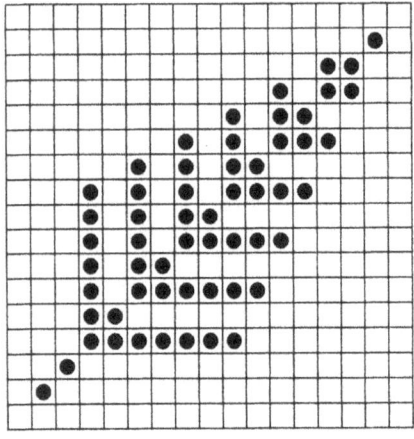

22

23

24

25

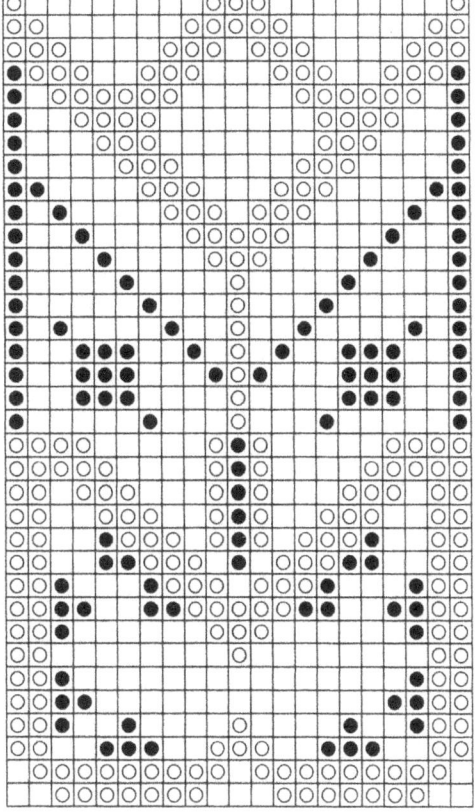

26

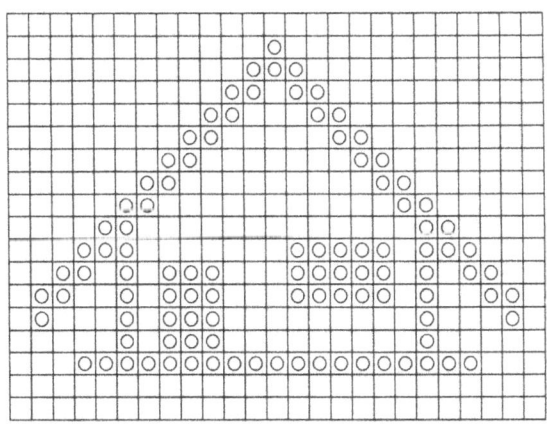

27

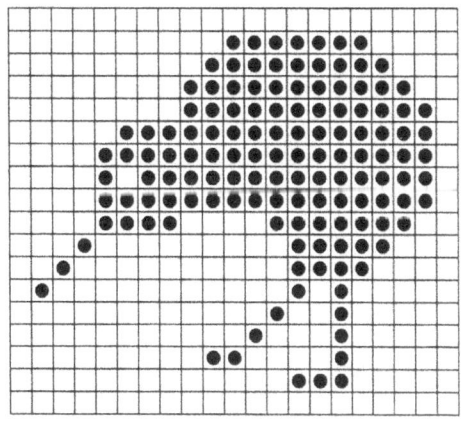

28

7

General Conclusions

While it is true that this study of tāniko has attempted to trace the history and development of this local art form from the time of Cook's first visit to New Zealand in 1769 up to the present time, its major emphasis has really been directed at the social context of art. A major premise of this work is that art is a cultural activity that cannot be fully understood in terms of itself. It is part of the total culture and it is intimately interlaced with other parts of the totality. Thus it is only by a many-sided study of the problem that we are likely to discover all the facts relevant to tāniko. Here, we have dealt with history, technological and social changes, style and fashion, ritual, classification, function and present-day context. These are the areas that I have considered to be important.

The traditional tāniko technique has been described in detail showing the materials used, how these were prepared, rolled into fibre and then dyed. The development of the technique has been discussed and analysed as a local development from the single-pair twine common to other areas of Polynesia. Although logically the tāniko weave can be viewed as an extension of the single-pair twine, the impetus leading to its discovery probably arose out of the attempt to duplicate basketry patterns as ornamentation for display cloaks.

In the chapter on history and development we examined the changing nature of tāniko through three time periods — the Classical, Transitional and Modern. The analysis of tāniko through these three periods for which we have documentary evidence led to the discovery of an identifiable sequence of change.

The first change from the Classical model was the addition of intrusive weaving material for decorative purposes. This immediately altered and extended the colour range in patterns. Efflorescence followed, with borders becoming wider and patterns more profuse. Intrusive motifs entered, first as only minor additions, and then as major sequences with in a continuing pattern but never completely displacing the Classical model. Wool was adopted then discarded as a weft material, and for a time there was a brief return to flax-based weaving threads. Then, new weaving materials were tried out — macramé twine and fishing line for warps, and coloured silks for wefts. After nearly 200 years of contact, the tāniko technique is gradually displaced by tapestry weaving. With the abandonment of traditional weaving materials and technique, what is left are the pattern motifs and certain arrangements of them. Thus patterns are very resistant to change.

The Classical inventory of motifs still forms the foundation of modern patterns. In spite of the fact that intrusive motifs may be used, the pattern arrangement as a whole tends to be Classical in conception. On present evidence the stability of pattern arrangements in decorative art seems to rank with the longevity of musical note arrangements in a particular culture. In his *Anthropology of Music*, Merriam stated that in spite of the phenomenon of change, 'There is some evidence... which points dramatically to the stability of music over time.'[1] I assume here that an arrangement of motifs to form a complete pattern is a culture trait similar to the arrangement of the notes which make up a song. A change in motifs here and there is similar to a change in musical notes at various points in the song. Such changes, however, are subsidiary to the general composition, which tends to persist through time.

The analysis of change in tāniko also led us to discuss what is most fundamental in a cultural artefact. In the case of tāniko the last thing still to change is the form of the patterns.

What is left after this stage, in any artefact, is an idea of its form, its cultural function and significance, and a certain nostalgia that lingers in the mind. Under the influence of social pressure the culture bearer of the idea may be prompted into recapturing its form in whatever material is at hand. However, when the idea is objectified, and supposing there are no genuine objects to use as models, the creator gives to it his or her own interpretation and so further change is introduced. I believe this is essentially what happens when innovative 'weavers' make impressions of cloaks.

A discussion of style brings out more dramatically the changes that tāniko has undergone. The sequence of change is not quite a one-way thing; some items come and go. But it is true to say that when an item reappears it is in a modified form so that style does follow a developmental path, no phase of it being quite the same as another. This is borne out by the different phases of the Classical style tradition we described. Many students of tāniko will be unfamiliar with the Pre-classic style, which is presented here for the first time. Its highly complex nature will surprise those who believe that the early stages of a particular art form ought to look primitively simple. As the evidence here will make clear, the Pre-classic style is not simple, but it presents tāniko in the frame of an entirely different style. I believe that such a phenomenon is best understood in terms of the style concept.

In the Modern period we found tāniko style had split into two: one conservative, in that the weavers who follow it resist change and aim at maintaining the Transitional style; the other progressive, in so far as weavers continue to adopt innovations. The two styles exist side by side, each serving a different set of purposes. In between these extremes are many weavers who follow an in-between course but who in fact oscillate from one style to the other depending on the demands of their clients. An interpretation placed on the facts observed here is that such fragmentation of style into high and low divisions marks the beginning of the decline and fall of the Classical style tradition. While the conservatives engage in a holding action, the modems will continue to experiment and innovate, ultimately pioneering a new conception of tāniko, which will still be founded on elements of the old. During the process of transition to a new style it will be necessary for progressive weavers to change the value system in favour of the new style so that it can become fashionable.

Since the rewriting of this book in 1973 and the revised edition of 1999, changes continued to affect tāniko. The position then was that the weavers were divisible into two categories. The traditional weavers worked with the traditional techniques and some insisted on using only traditional materials. This section of the traditional weavers revived old techniques and incorporated tikanga, that is, the customary practices associated with weaving. The women following this development tended to be experimentalists and researchers as the task they set themselves required reviving old techniques. They tended also to be very talented. Dame Rangimarie Hetet led the movement and set very high standards.

The other section among traditional weavers did not mind using modern materials in the purses, belts and other objects they made. Whatever the materials used, however, the weaving technique used was that of finger weaving, or tāniko.

The innovative group experimented with other weaving techniques and introduced the tapestry weave, which became very popular.

By 1997, the two groups could still be identified but some of the younger weavers are now experimenting with both traditional techniques and with modern innovations. In other words, they have an experimental attitude to weaving. They may combine several weaving techniques, include plaiting and feather work, and experiment with new materials. They are familiar with traditional techniques and materials but at this stage of their careers have not settled upon a clear preference for traditional or innovative weaving.

The innovative group of the past turned to tradition for their inspiration. Abandoned techniques from traditional times are brought back into use, but not in the same context as before. New combinations are created and new objects are being exhibited. It is an exciting development that is inspiring some weavers, male and female, to create beautiful examples of weaving. This movement is innovative and creative and yet remains true to the weaving traditions of the past.

It is noticeable in the 1990s that tāniko patterns are more in evidence than ever before. Tāniko as an art form is not dying, quite the opposite. Weavers are finding new

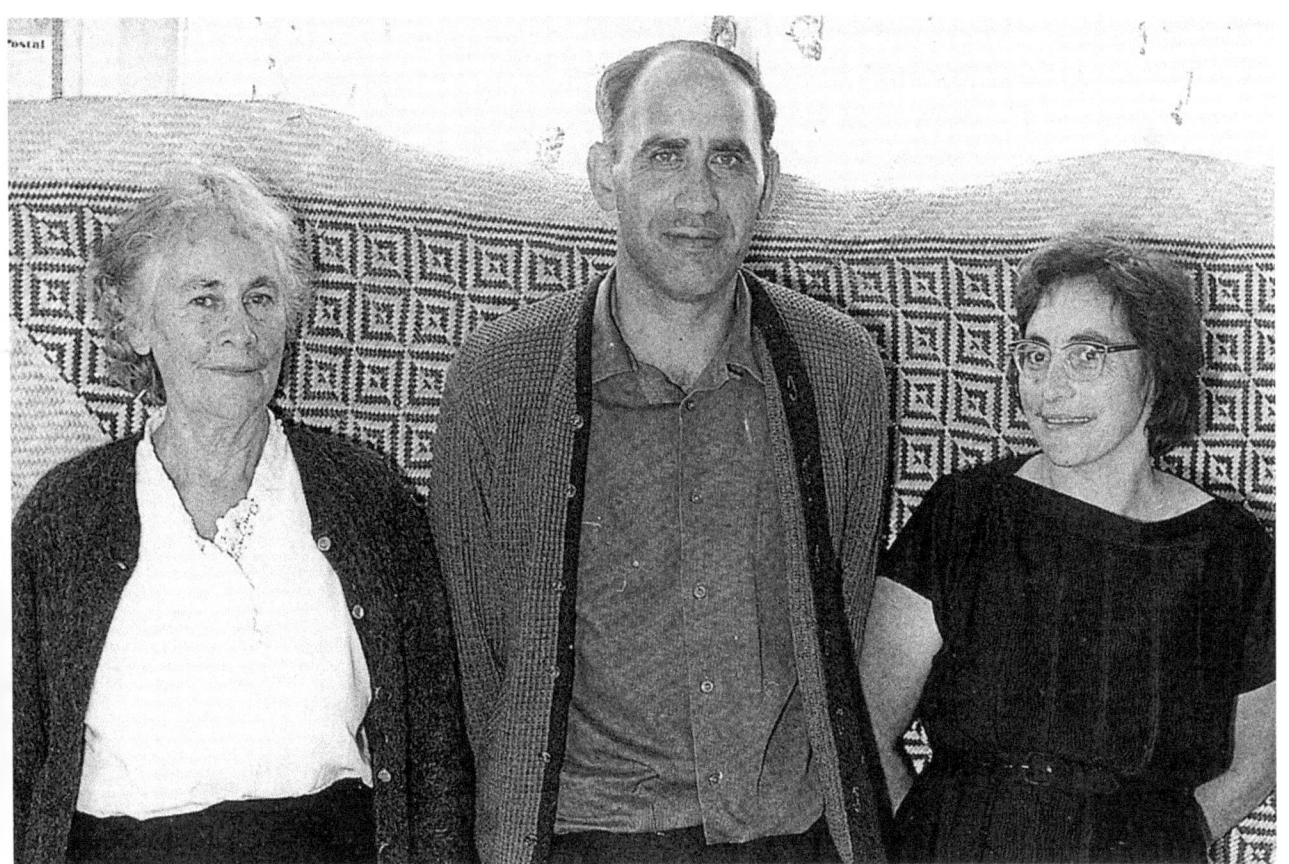

Dame Rangimarie Hetet of Te Kuiti (left) with her daughter, Mrs Digger Te Kanawa (right), and the author, Te Kuiti, 1965.

C.A. Schollum

ways of applying tāniko patterns. In the case of piupiu, an essential part of the costume required for the performing arts, the tāniko band is becoming wider, especially in the Rotorua area, where I first noted this change at the Māori Art Institute in 1996.

Objects woven out of traditional materials and using the tāniko technique are highly valued as gifts. In some leather handbags a tāniko section is built into the design and this adds a different quality to an object that does not relate to traditional forms.

So in the approach to the year 2000, tāniko weaving remains a highly valued technique. The patterns separable from the weaving technique are not restricted to weaving. Tāniko patterns feature in several meeting houses of the Bay of Plenty region. For example, in Mataatua, built in the period 1873-75 at Whakatane, tāniko patterns feature as the upper border of tukutuku panels and they appear right around the interior of a carved house. The patterns are easily transferable to other art forms and in this sense will not die out.

Although much has been written about style, considered as a social phenomenon by such important figures as Boas, Schapiro, Sapir and Kroeber, I believe the concept of style deserves a great deal more attention by investigators of art forms and material culture. We still know too little about the dynamics of style; the precise nature of the relationship between art style and social structure is largely unknown, although we have had impressions, hints and inspired guesses that have suggested how the relationship might work. In this book I have contributed my share of hints and impressions.

In the chapter on classification, an attempt was made to present a system that accounted for all known pattern arrangements in the present corpus. Using dominant motif as the criterion of class allocation, seven categories were set up. The system is an extension of Buck's 1911 classification, which was set up on the basis of internal cultural information.

Tāniko provides one vehicle, among others in the culture, by which and through which cultural ideas are expressed and objectified. It has been used both consciously and unconsciously by Māori to express their individuality as a people and to provide some visual, concrete manifestation of the concept of Māoritanga. The concept is regarded as a religious tenet by the majority of Māori; one need only attend important social functions and listen to the speeches to get confirmation of the general importance given to it. In the modern context, Māoritanga is an organising principle that colours Māori behaviour and influences decision-making. It is at once the rationale for present cultural behaviour and the main motivation for future actions. Tāniko has a place within this conceptual scheme; thus, I believe that it will survive though continuing to undergo change.

A certain quality of Māori society comes through in the history of tāniko, and this is the refusal of its members as a group to go all the way in the matter of change. Even though they are apparently perfectly willing to innovate and experiment, a line is drawn at a certain point. Within this line is a cultural residue they will protect and maintain at all costs. This is the cultural germ that gives them their individuality, and without it they would become a characterless minority within New Zealand society. From present evidence it seems certain that Māori society will maintain itself in the future, and that it will not become submerged by the larger society.

Notes
1. Merriam, 1964, p. 304.

8

Instructions for Learning Tāniko Weaving

Part 1 Making a sampler

Instructions on learning the tāniko technique are based on the construction of one small sampler.

Alternative methods are dealt with later so as not to cause any confusion. It is assumed that after making the sampler and after some practise with alternative methods, the beginner will be able to go ahead and weave larger articles.

Materials required: one ball of macramé twine (or thick binding twine), two hanks of knitting silk of contrasting colours (white and black, or red and black, and so on), graph paper, pencil, eraser, scissors.

Preparation of the pattern

1. Once the beginner has become more familiar with tāniko one should create new patterns rather than copy old ones. Freehand drawings can be made of various pattern arrangements until a suitable one is finally settled on.

2. The freehand drawing can now be translated onto graph paper. Each square on the graph here illustrated represents a point where a weft thread crosses a warp. A decision has to be made at this stage as to what the black cross or circle on the

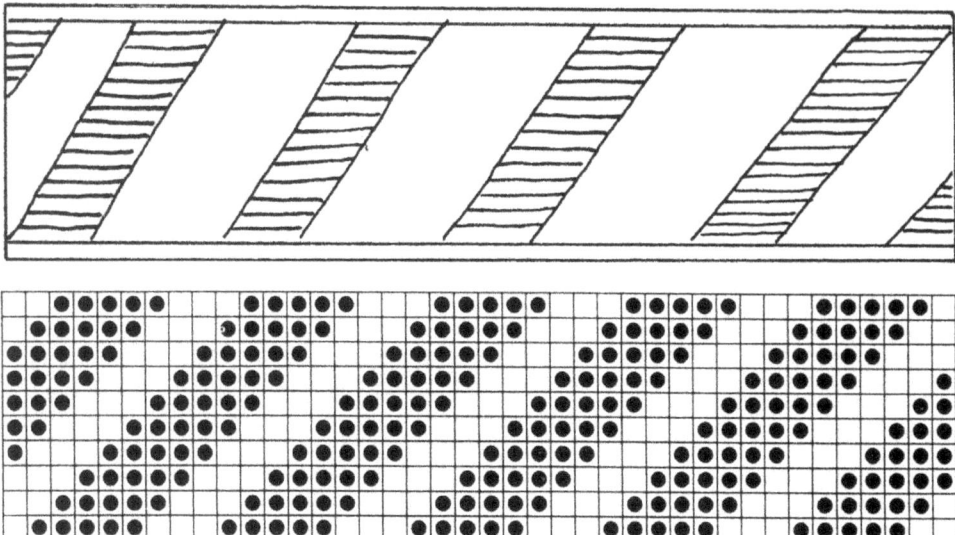

A freehand drawing of the pattern and the pattern on graph paper.

graph is to mean. Is it to represent black, which is the background of the pattern, or is it to represent the contrasting colour? In the sampler graph illustrated here, black circles stand for black, and empty spaces stand for white. Reference to the graph will reveal a number of facts, for example, the number of weft rows for the pattern itself (10 in this case) and the number of warps, which, because of the casting-on technique, must always be an even number. Every warp element added is folded to make two. As a rule an odd number of weft rows gives the best results, especially for patterns required to be continued downwards.

3. Read off numbers and sequence of colour from the graph and arrange as shown.
B = black thread **W** = white thread

Note Most experienced weavers read directly from the graph as they work, but even they sometimes make mistakes. I recommend that the beginner works from the sequence table, which can be checked periodically by reference to the graph.

ROW														
Sequence Table: order and number of colours														
1	4B	3W	5B	3W	5B	3W	5B	3W	5B	3W	5B	—	—	—
2	3B	3W	5B	3W	5B	3W	5B	3W	5B	3W	5B	1W	—	—
3	2B	3W	5B	3W	5B	3W	5B	3W	5B	3W	5B	2W	—	—
4	1B	3W	5B	3W	5B	3W	5B	3W	5B	3W	5B	3W	—	—
5	—	3W	5B	3W	5B	3W	5B	3W	5B	3W	5B	3W	1B	—
6	—	2W	5B	3W	5B	3W	5B	3W	5B	3W	5B	3W	2B	—
7	—	1W	5B	3W	5B	3W	5B	3W	5B	3W	5B	3W	3B	—
8	—	—	5B	3W	5B	3W	5B	3W	5B	3W	5B	3W	4B	—
9	—	—	5B	3W	5B	3W	5B	3W	5B	3W	5B	3W	5B	—
10	—		5B	3W	5B	3W	5B	3W	5B	3W	5B	3W	5B	1W

This table shows the weaving sequence for each row of the sampler.

Part 2 Preparation of warps and wefts

Cut 30 8-centimetre lengths of macramé twine or thick string. These are your warps.

Cut a length of white silk 40 centimetres long and the same length of black silk. These are the wefts.

When preparing large numbers of warps it is a good idea to find some object like a medicine bottle, the circumference of which is equal or nearly equal to the length of one warp, in this case 8 centimetres. Wind the macramé around this object and cut along one side. In this way you mass-produce the warps.

Part 3 Casting on; the fixing process

The casting-on process attaches all warp elements together to form the upper selvedge of the article. The double wefts used here are called the *two-pair interlocking weft* or twine, for reasons which will become apparent as the work proceeds. The technique is basic to cloak making as well as tāniko. What follows is one way of casting on. There are others.

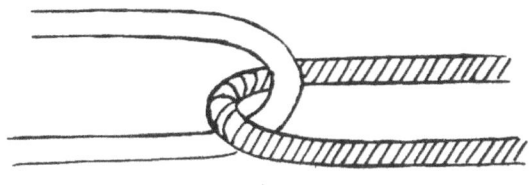

I Double white and black wefts and link together.

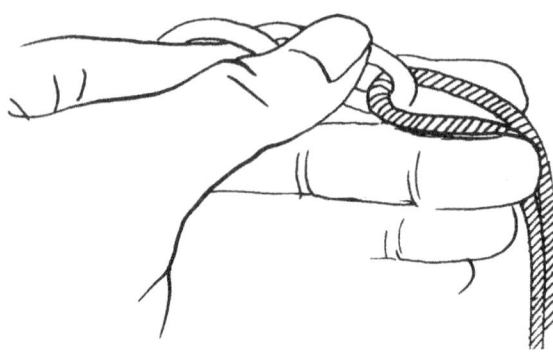

2 Hold in the left hand.

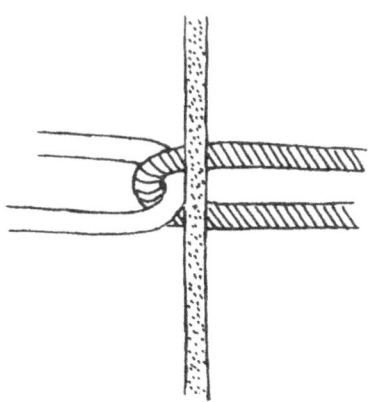

3 Place the first warp thread (8-centimetre macramé) over the black threads, making sure that the middle of the warp is lying across the black wefts.

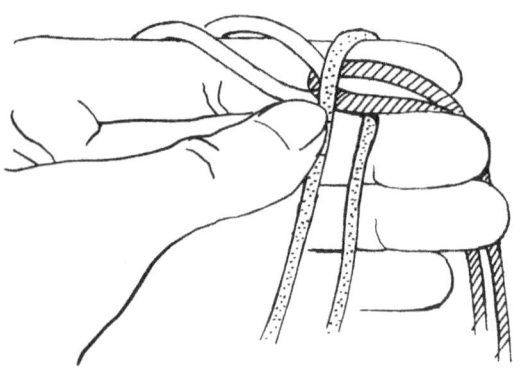

4 Bend the upper end of the warp back and bring it through between forefinger and middle finger. Hold it in that position.

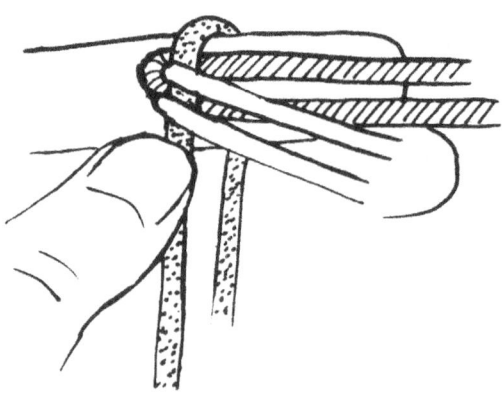

5 With the right hand pick up the white weft threads and transfer to the right of the warp.

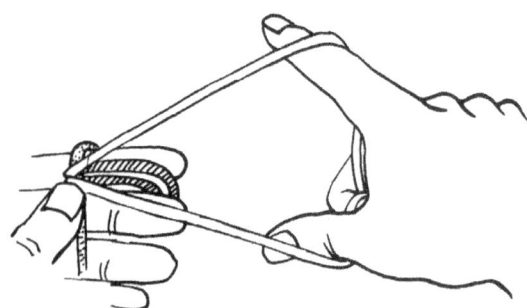

6 Hold the white wefts in the right hand leaving the thumb and forefinger free. Now place thumb and forefinger down in between the two whites.

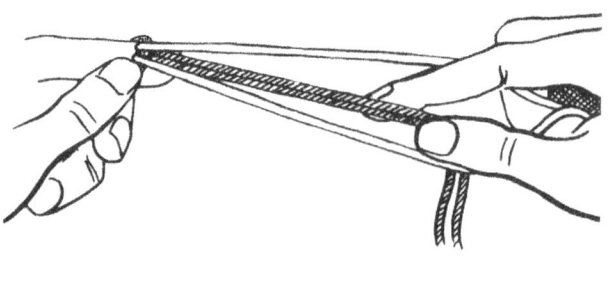

7 With the thumb and forefinger take hold of the black weft threads and bring them up through the whites (as shown in diagram) at the same time dropping the whites.

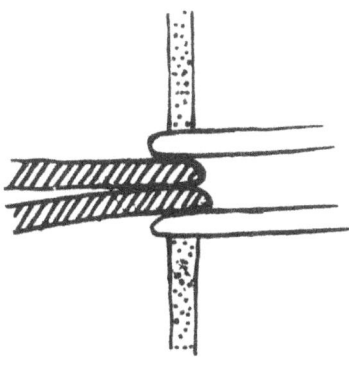

8 Carry the blacks over to the left side of warp to original position of white. The wefts have now changed places.

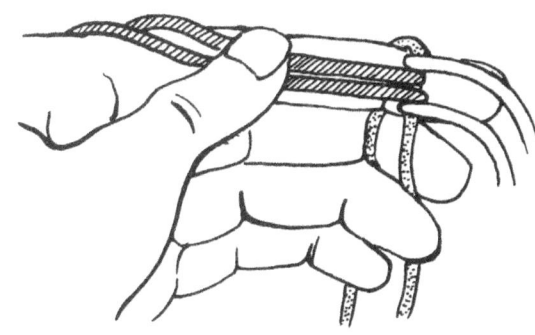

9 Hold as shown and this will free the right hand.

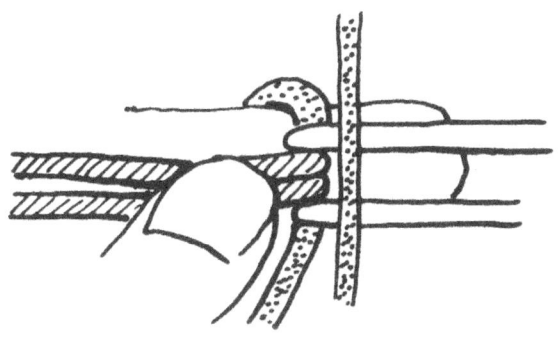

10 Place the second warp into position, this time over the white threads. Bend upper end down as for first warp.

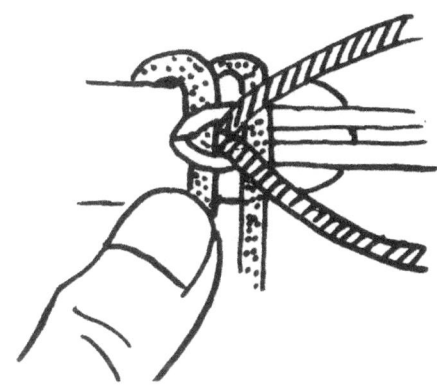

11 Bring black weft threads over the repeat figures 6 and 7.

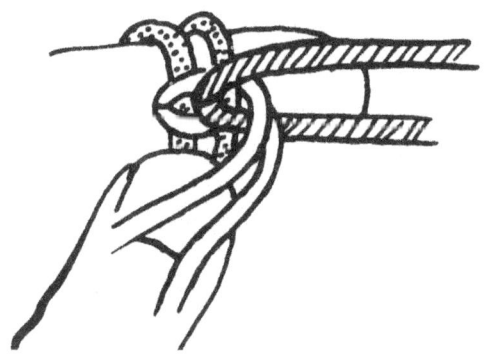

12 The result of these moves is shown.

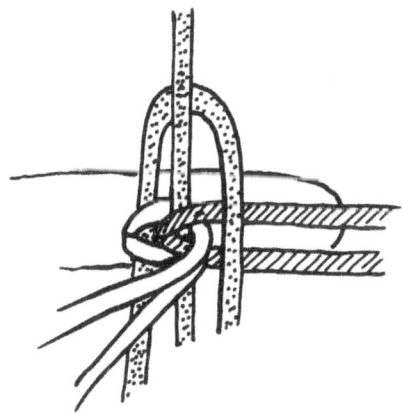

13 Release the two upper ends of the warps from the forefinger and middle finger grip. Turn upper end of first warp behind second warp and down over black wefts. Repeat 5, 6 and 7.

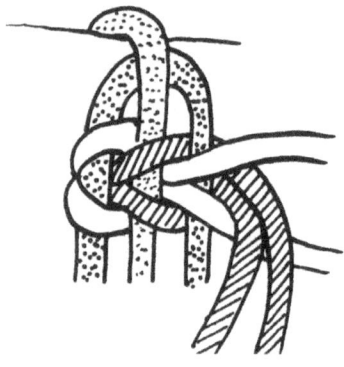

14 This is the position now reached.

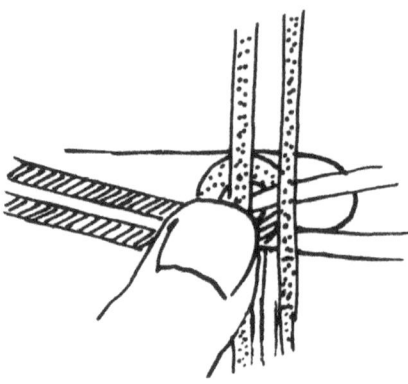

15 Place the third warp over the white wefts.

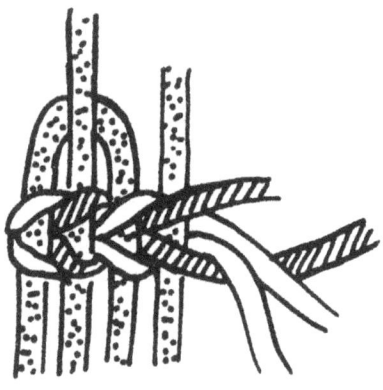

16 'Fix' this one in by repeating 5, 6 and 7.

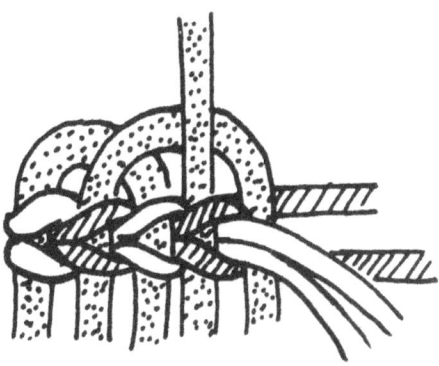

17 Release upper ends of second and third warps. Bring the upper end of the second warp behind third warp and down over the wefts. 'Fix' in by repeating 5, 6 and 7.

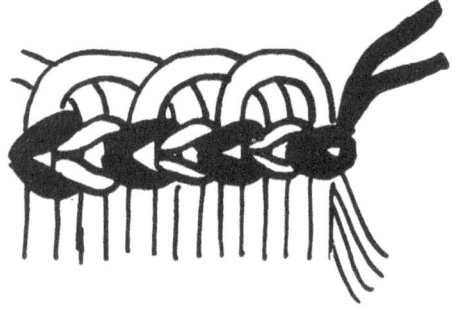

18 The last warp is not fixed in the usual way, but is simply tied in by tying the two pairs of wefts into a reef knot. The rest is now a matter of repeating 15, 16 and 17 until the end is reached.

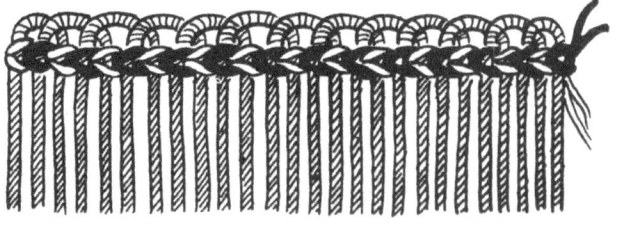

19 A diagrammatic picture of what our article should look like when the casting on is completed

Part 4 The tāniko weave; the actual weaving of the pattern

In my earlier book I called this section *twisting* because the action is essentially one of twisting weft threads and twisting the wrist. Buck called the technique the *wrapped twine* because, for him, the basic action seemed to be one of wrapping threads. I have decided to call this traditionally based technique simply the *tāniko weave*. Some purists might object to the use of the term weave, but it is, as you will see, a form of simple hand weaving. As you work the two-pair interlocking weft you will notice that you are actually changing sheds with your fingers and wrist before bringing in the next warp. The tāniko weave is actually more of a weave than so called tapestry weaving; the latter belongs to the general craft of sewing.

The tāniko technique enables a weaver to carry as many as five colours along each weft row, bringing forward at will whichever colour is demanded by the pattern. In the sampler only two colours are used, but the principles are the same whether two, three or more colours are used. Rules 1 and 2, mentioned later in this section, embody these principles.

We are here preparing two lots of weft threads. One lot (a black and a white) will be used for the first row of the design while the other will be ready for the second row. This is purely a time-saving method and, incidentally, a neater one. You could, if you so desired, prepare one row at a time by tying the two ends together.

The twisting of the linked weft threads is to prevent them from slipping when the first warp is twisted into place.

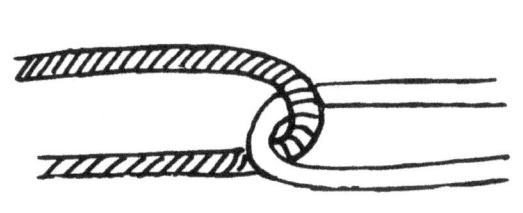

I Cut 60-centimetre lengths of black and white silk threads and link them.

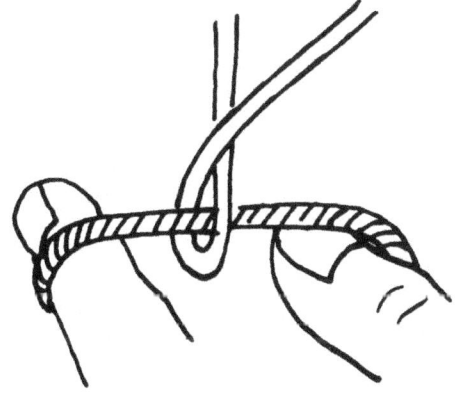

2 Hold black thread about the middle with forefinger and thumb of left hand.

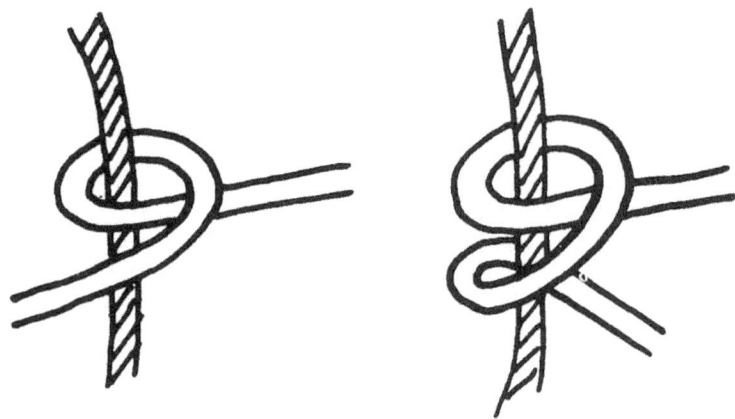

3 and 4 Hold white in right hand and twist as shown.

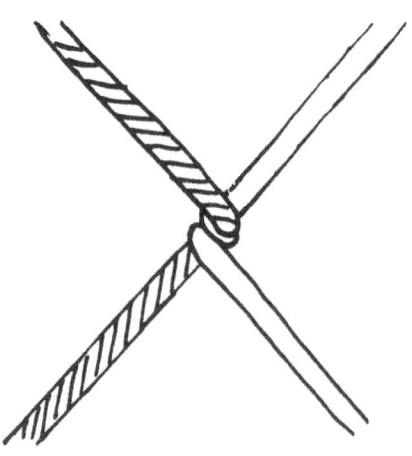

5 Pull threads to tighten the grip.

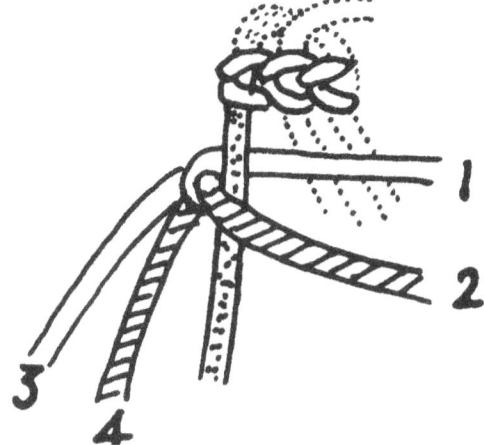

6 Bring the first warp into place, making sure that it lies over the white and under the black, because black is the colour we want shown. (Refer to graphed design or to number chart.)

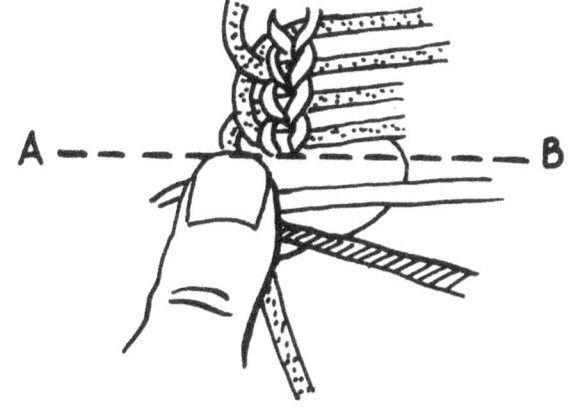

7 Push the wefts right up against the casting-on weft row and hold with thumb and forefinger of left hand.

Note In the diagrams following figure 7 all that section above the AB in figure 7 is left out for the sake of clarity. Let your imagination add that portion to the rest.

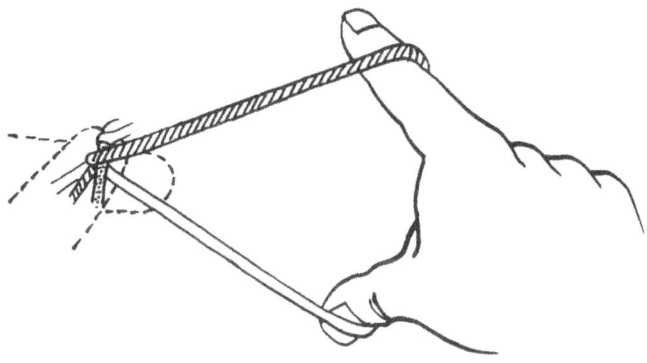

8 Position One. Place the black thread over the forefinger of the left hand and the white under the thumb. This will be referred to now as Position One. In this position the right-hand palm is facing out from the body.

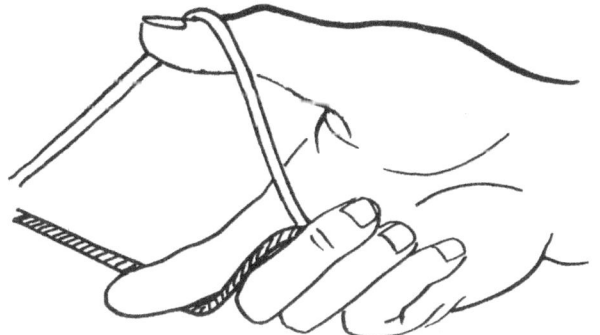

9 Position Two. Now rotate the palm of the right hand away from the body, towards the floor (clockwise) until the palm is facing upwards. This is Position Two. The palm now is towards the body and facing upward. The rotation of the hand from the wrist covers half a circle and this represents what we shall term a 'twist'. It will be obvious, of course, that the hand is incapable of making a complete circle.

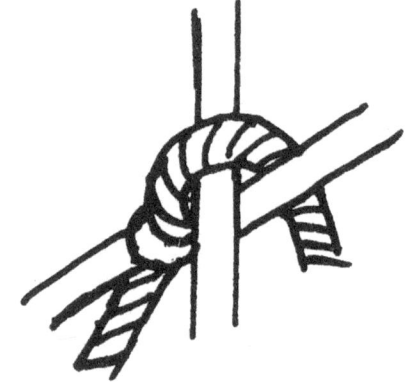

10 Remove thumb and forefinger from the wefts and insert again between threads, from body-side outwards so as to arrive at Position One again. As a result of the half-turn, the forefinger now carries the white and the thumb carries the black.

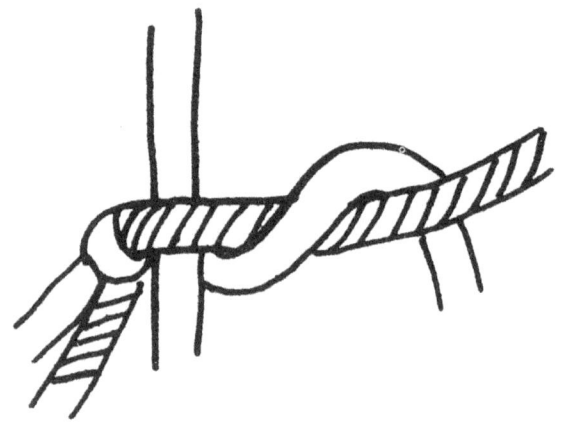

11 Repeat the movements from Position One to Position Two. You have now made two twists or a complete revolution of the hand in two stages. The second twist brings the black up and (if you remember) black is the colour required by our design to show over warp two.

Refer again to 10 and 11. Here you will see what the two twists actually do. Compare your effort with the diagrams.

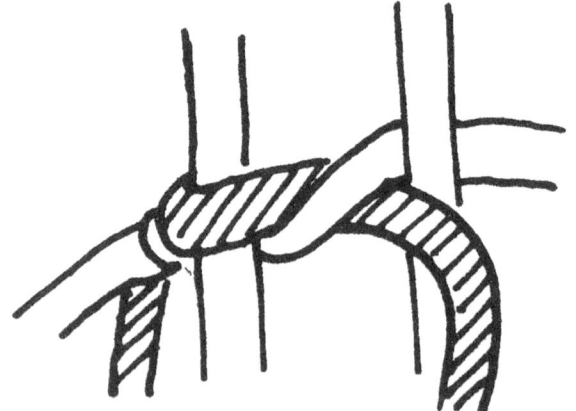

12 Bring the next warp into place, making sure that it lies over the white and under the black weft as illustrated.

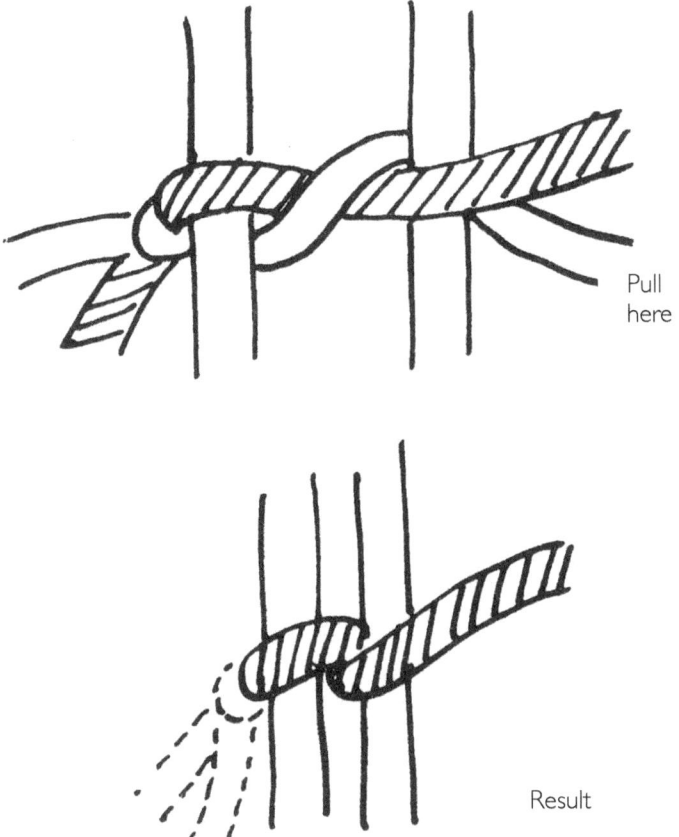

Pull
here

Result

13 and 14 Hold second warp down with thumb and forefinger of left hand and pull the white tightly so that only the black shows at the front.

This is extremely important and I want you to take careful note of what this does. If the black is pulled instead, it is obvious that the white would show. The rule is: when tightening wefts, always pull the bottom weft.

Repeat Position One to Position Two twice, that is, twist twice over the second warp to bring black up again.

Bring third warp into place.

Tighten previous one by pulling white.

Twist wefts twice to fasten third warp in.

Bring fourth warp into place and tighten the previous one by pulling black.

I must now leave you on your own, as the rest is simply a matter of repetition.

However, for your guidance here are two rules in connection with the twists.

Rule 1 — to bring the same colour up again, twist twice.

Rule 2 — to change colour, twist once only. When you reach the end of each row, tie the ends of the wefts with a reef knot.

General Notes on Part 4

1 When the first row is completed begin the second, the threads for which you have ready. (Figure 6, threads 3 and 4).

2 After completing the second row, prepare wefts for the next two rows, as shown, and so on, until you have done the required 10 rows.

3 You have probably noticed that some tāniko belts have three colours and not just two. To work three colours prepare a three-colour weft row the same way as you have been shown for a two-colour one, and when twisting bring up the colour you want the usual way and use the other two for tightening.

4 Some people have a tighter twist than others, thus producing a closer and stiffer fabric. You must determine your own tension. It is, however, better to twist a little tighter than a little too loose.

The Last Two Rows

Although the actual design contains only 10 rows you will find that you have actually 12 rows by the time you complete the tenth row of the design — two rows were put on during the casting on. To balance the design, therefore, we must add another two rows in the same manner as the first two. Now, refer back to the casting-on diagrams on pages 101–104.

a Prepare double threads as in 1 and hold as in 2 on pages 101–102.

b Bring end of first warp over black as in 4 on page 102.

c Repeat stages up to 9 on pages 102–103.

d Bring end of second warp over the white as in 10 on page 103.

e Fix in as for first warp.

f Repeat the above until the last warp is reached. End this off the same way as in the casting on.

g You are now ready to cast off.

There is no alternative method for the tāniko weave. However, you may discover better ways of attaching different-coloured threads together, preferably without the use of knots. To help keep the work straight and tight, some weavers use an extra weft thread in each row; this is called a passive thread. Its function is to pull the work together every now and then. When it is realised that the greatest problem in tāniko is keeping the work straight and even, the function of this passive thread will be fully appreciated. All the passive rows together provide the weaver with a means of making final adjustments to the article. The use of passive threads date back to the Classical period.

When working with several colours it is often much easier simply to add the required colour and carry it as a passive thread until it is needed. When it has been used, take it along for at least a sufficient distance to tie it in effectively, then cut it off. By using this technique any number of colours may be used in a pattern.

It is possible to use one colour and still show a pattern. This is done by varying either the thickness or the tension of the weave.

Part 5 Casting off

The method outlined here is easy, but it is not the best one for neatest results. It is recommended that you come to grips as soon as possible with alternative method B described in part 7. Turn the article upside down so that the hanging warps are at the top and the inside is facing your body.

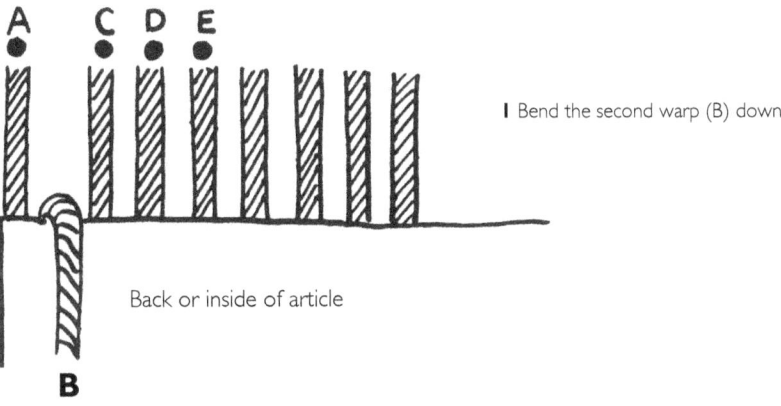

1 Bend the second warp (B) down.

Back or inside of article

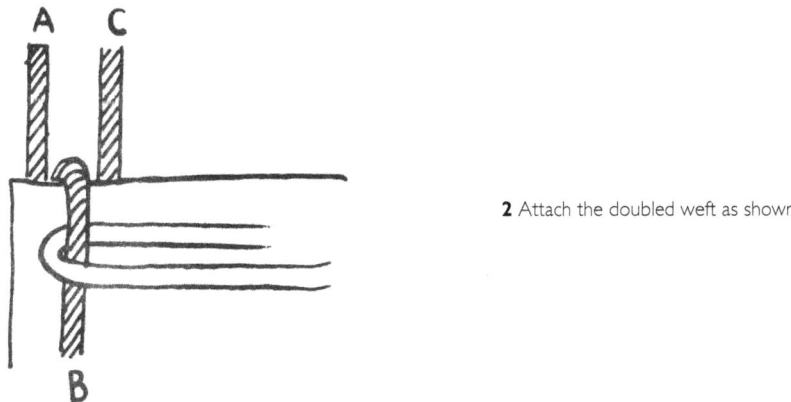

2 Attach the doubled weft as shown.

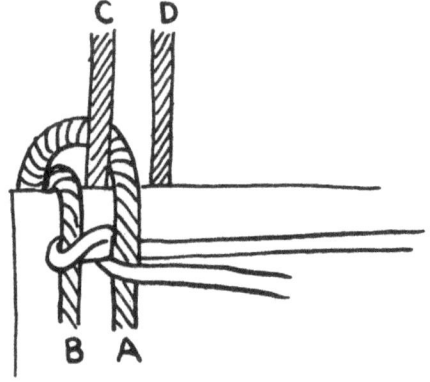

3 Apply a single twist. B end warp A over behind warp C and down in between wefts. Fix this in with a single twist.

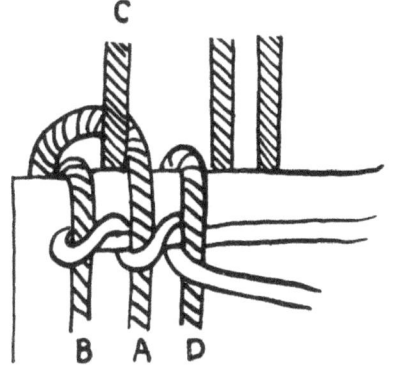

4 Bend warp D down and fix with a single twist.

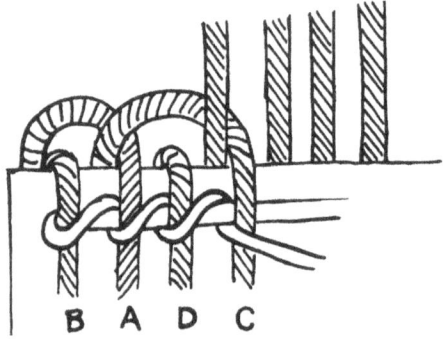

5 Bend C over, behind E and in between wefts. Fix this in the usual way.

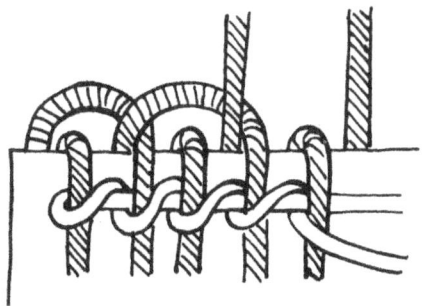

6 The rest is now a matter of repetition. Figure 6 gives the next stage from which you should be able to continue on your own.

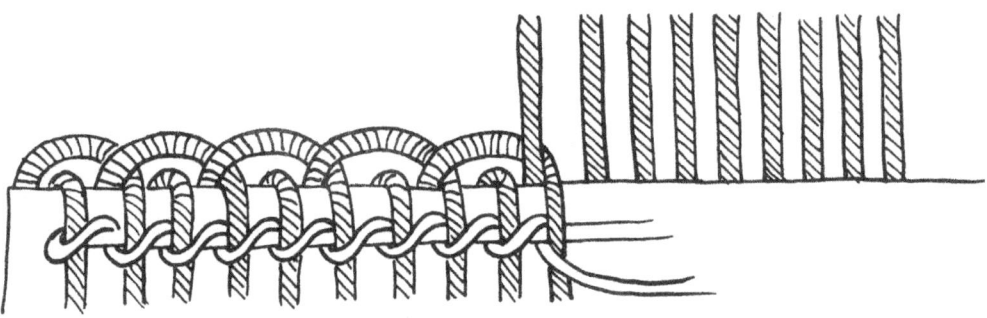

7 The pattern of the warps caused by the casting off is shown in this diagram.

When the last warp has been fixed into place tie the loose weft ends together with a reef knot.

This completes the actual tāniko weaving, although there still remains one more task before our sampler assumes that 'finished ' look. That final task is to line or cover the inside with a strip of cloth or leather. Instructions for backing tāniko articles are given in another chapter.

Nowadays most tāniko weavers take their belts to a saddler to be lined with leather, but you could quite easily do your own.

Before closing this section here are two facts that may help you when planning future tāniko articles.

a   When using macramé twine and knitting silk, about 10 warps are required for every 2 centimetres

b   About 10 weft rows are required to each centimetre.

It often happens, however, that macramé twine varies in thickness, in which case the above facts would not be too reliable. The number of wefts to the centimetre depends on the tension you use and on the thickness of the silk or wool, although the silk varies very little, if at all.

Now that you have been right through the various stages of this sampler you should be able to make a tāniko belt or some other article on your own. Only experience can teach you the finer points of the craft.

Part 6 Alternative methods of casting on

In the method illustrated one doubled thread is used instead of the pair used for the sampler. A study of these diagrams will show you what was done. After figure 12 many variations are possible, although few are practicable.

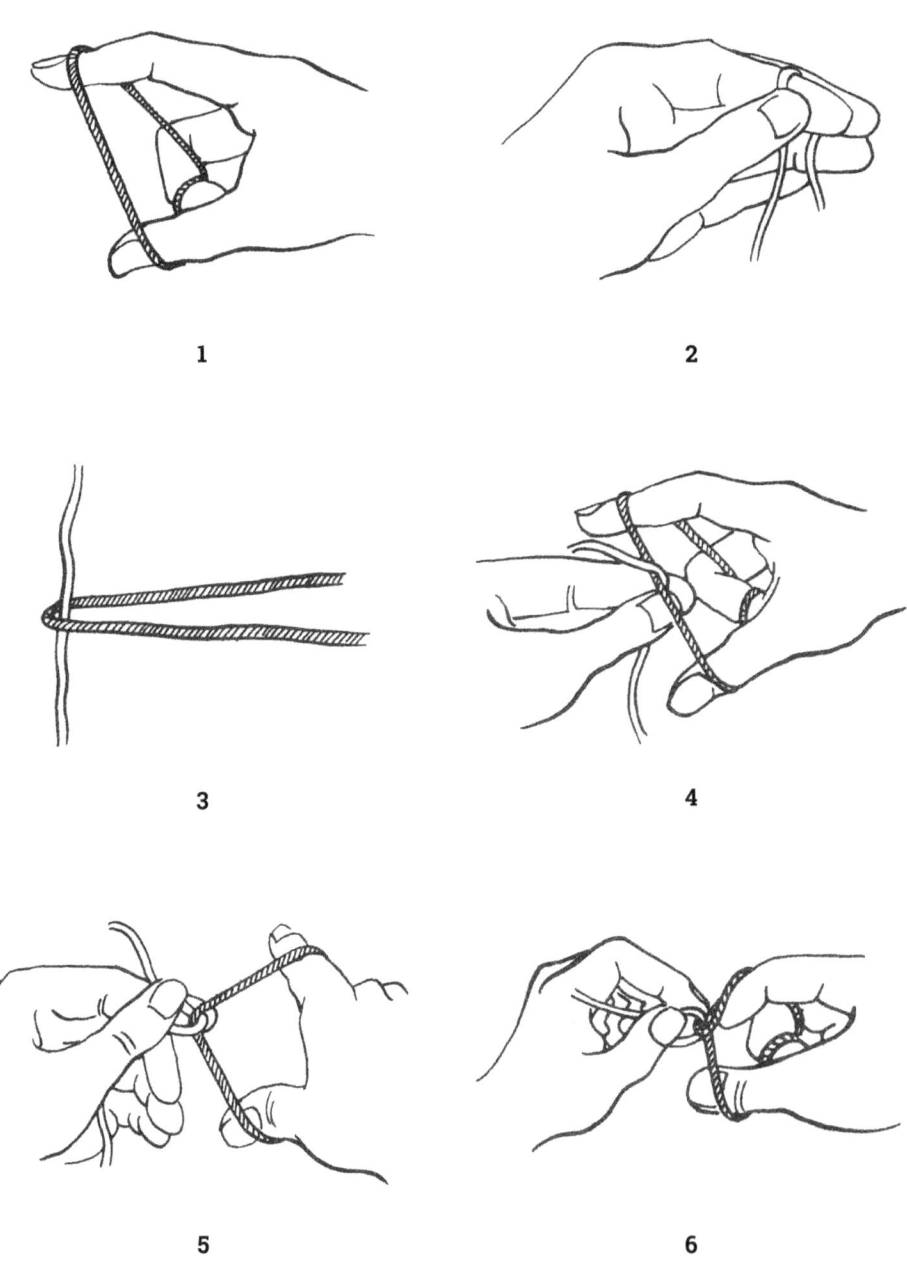

1

2

3

4

5

6

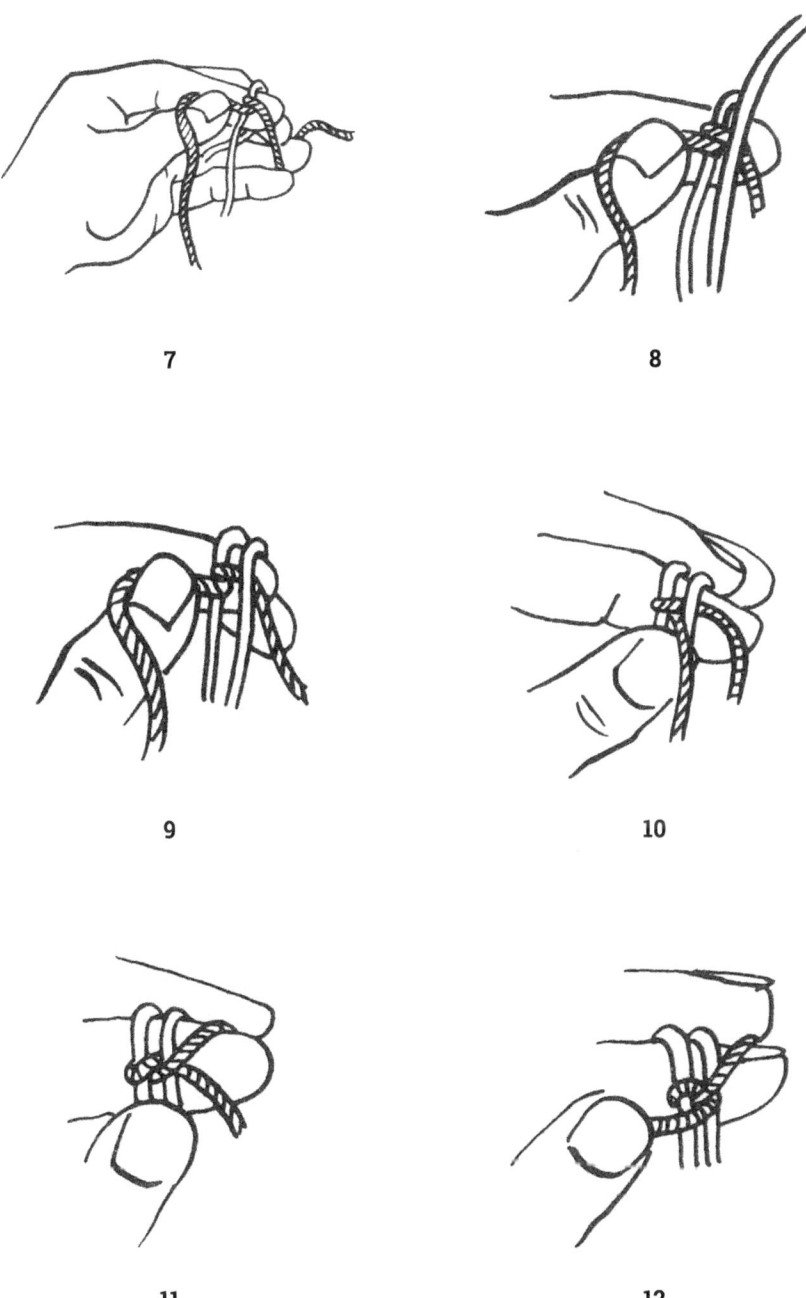

7

8

9

10

11

12

Method A

Diagrams 1, 2 and 3 below show the three stages in this method of casting on. The top end of the first warp is turned over after fixing in the second warp.

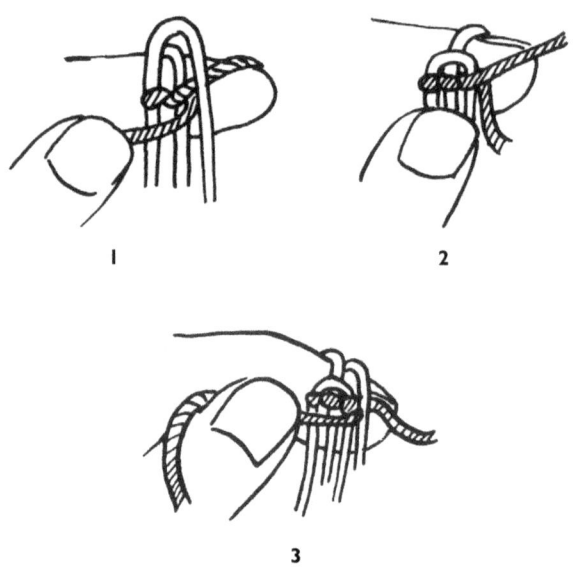

Method B

In this method, the top end of the first warp is turned over after fixing the third as shown in the three stages above. You may also turn the first over, after fixing the fourth one, but you need to experiment to find the one that suits your tastes. The casting-on method used for the sampler may be varied the same way.

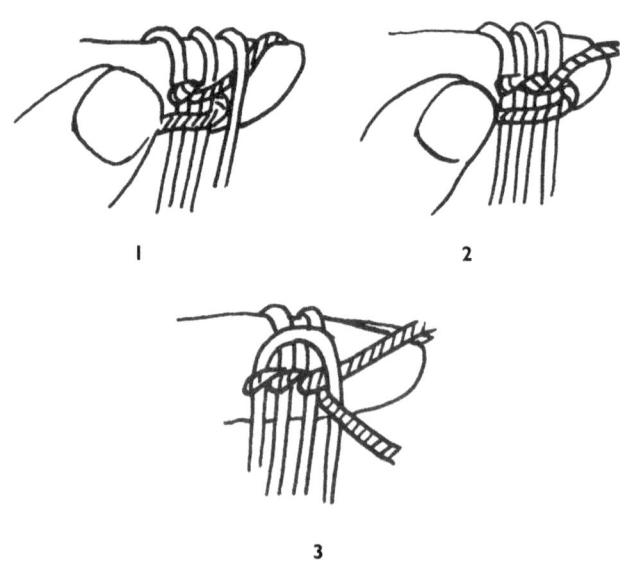

Part 7 Alternative methods of casting off

Two other methods are shown here.

Method A

Method A is by far the easiest method of casting off, but, unfortunately, it is not the neatest; thus not many people use it. No weft element is used; the warps are interwoven in such a way as to keep themselves in place. Refer now to the diagrams which explain themselves. The article is turned upside-down as before. Some indication of the pattern formed by the warps is given in figure 5. When the last warp is reached, turn it down and tie as shown in figure 6 with the loose ends of the last weft row.

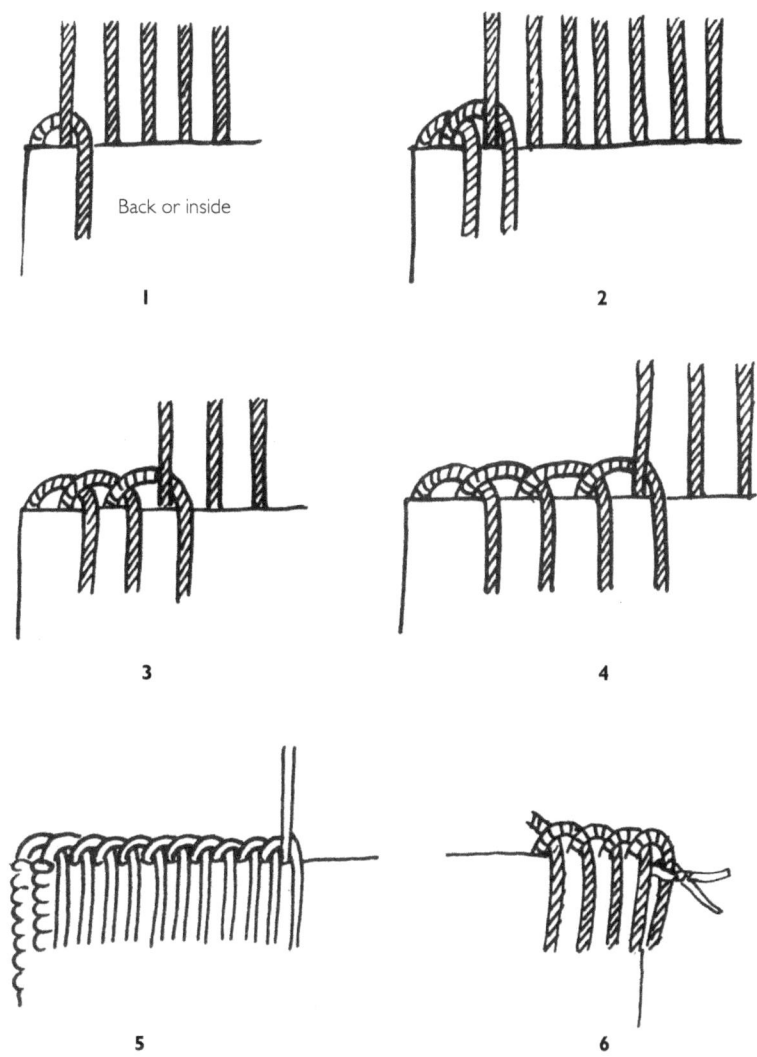

Back or inside

1

2

3

4

5

6

Method B

Method B looks a bit more difficult but will save much time because you put on the last two rows (refer to page 110) and cast off in the same operation. Prepare the doubled pair of wefts and link together as you have been shown.

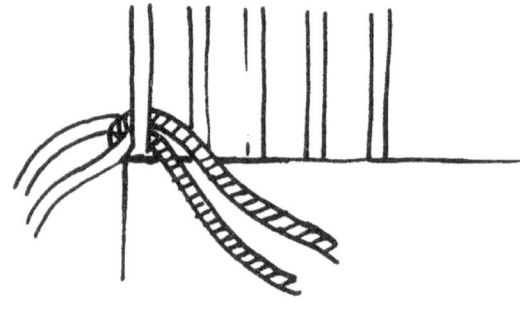

1 Turn the article upside-down so that the warp ends are at the top.

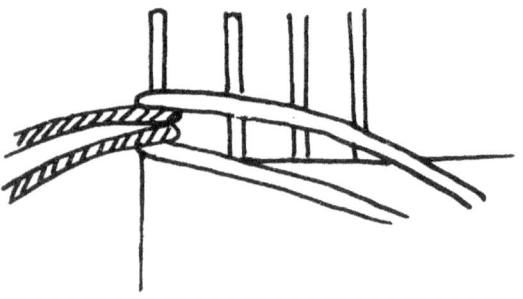

2 Place the wefts around the first warp and fix this in (as 5, 6, 7, 8 and 9 on pages 102–103) as shown.

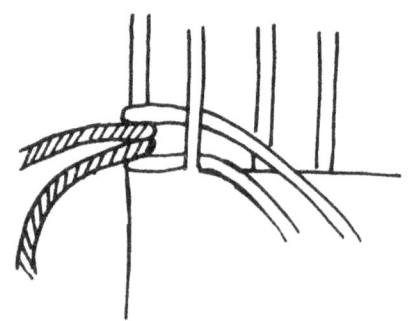

3 Bring second warp into place.

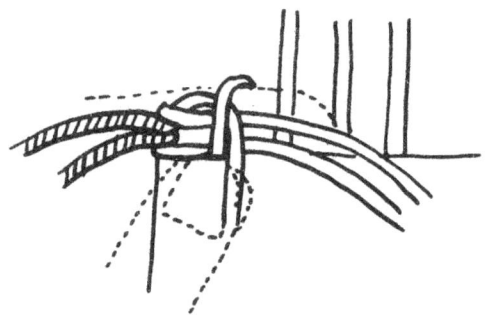

4 Now turn end of first warp over behind the second and down over wefts. This is held by the left hand as shown by the dots, thus leaving the right hand free.

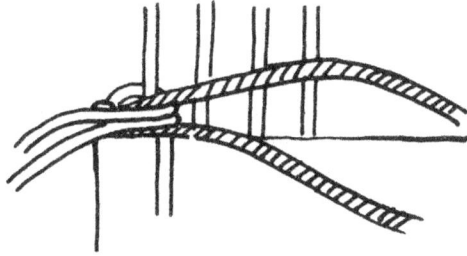

5 Now fix these two in together.

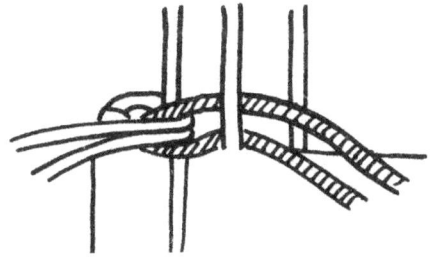

6 The rest is now a matter of repetition. The third warp is put into place.

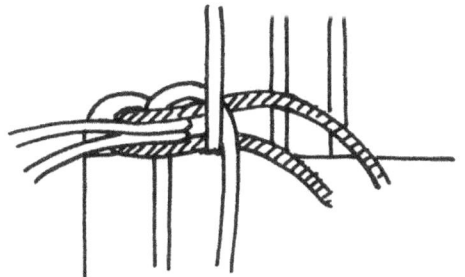

7 The end of the second is turned over behind this and down over the wefts.

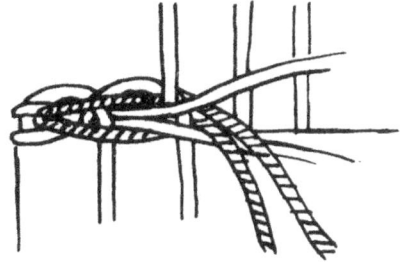

8 Fix these two, and so on.

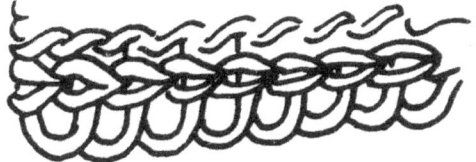

9 The pattern as formed on the outside of the article is shown here. You will recognise that the last two rows correspond with the first.

No matter what method you use for casting off, the ends of the warps must be pulled down evenly afterwards. You may have to repeat this operation several times before you arrive at a satisfactory finish.

Part 8 Making a tāniko belt

If you have successfully mastered the sampler you may feel confident enough to try a tāniko belt. It would be tedious to give detailed instruction on how to make a belt, as we did for the sampler. The thing to do now is to apply what you have learnt. However, these following few hints may be helpful.

1   Make all wefts half as long again as the length of the belt. This means that if the belt is to be 60 centimetres long, each doubled weft should be 90 centimetres long. At the time the future owner's waist is measured the weaver should already have decided the type of finish and attachment. Allow at least 10 centimetres for leather ends and buckle.
2   The double warps should be half as long again as the width of the article, and this is especially important in narrow bands, such as in belts.
3   Using standard macramé twine and silk wefts in a fairly loose weave, there will be approximately 16 weft rows to the inch; a tighter weave will take up 17 or 18 wefts. With this information, graphed patterns can be translated into width in centimetres.

4 With standard materials there will be approximately 10 to 12 warps to the inch

5 It is important to keep the work to an even tension; otherwise, the article will go so out of shape that nothing will straighten it. For this reason it is not a good idea to let every Tom, Dick and Harry have a few twists here and there.

6 Check and double check with the graphed pattern as you proceed. An error can go unnoticed for several weft rows, and the thought of undoing them is too much for some weavers.

7 A sequence table should be drawn up, but not for the whole belt; all that should be included are the main units of the pattern. This may be one, two or more, depending on the pattern selected. The advantage here is that you are not forever having to count and recount graphed squares.

8 As a rule, use an odd number of wefts for patterns required to be repeated in depth.

9 When the pattern has been completed and the casting off finished, stretch the belt to its full length and tack it down onto a piece of flat board. Leave it like this for a day.

10 If you are handy to a good saddler, take your belt there to be backed in leather and have a buckle fitted. If you prefer to do the lining yourself, part 9 will help you.

Part 9 Lining and finishing

Your belt is now ready for lining. This can be done with a variety of materials, but a thin leather is best, as this will not cling to your clothing but will slide easily. The leather must be thin to avoid giving the work a clumsy appearance, and for this reason skiver leather is the most suitable.

It can be obtained in a number of good shades, as well as a natural colour. Lining basil is another good material, and this is always in a natural shade.

These materials can be bought from any wholesalers of leather, but it would be necessary to purchase a whole skin. This is all right for schools, or where a number of

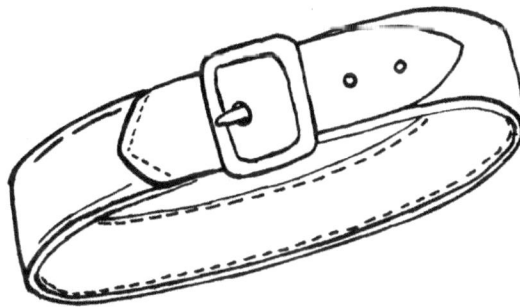

Your tāniko belt requires a leather lining as well as two leather ends and a buckle.

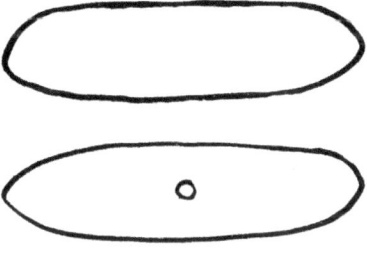

The bottom leather end has a hole punched to take the buckle.

students could share the skin. However, smaller pieces can usually be obtained from a saddler. Small pieces of thin calf or basil can also be obtained for attaching to the ends of the tāniko belt.

Finishing the ends

Cut leather for the belt ends according to the width of the belt and buckle. On the buckle end cut the leather twice the required length; punch a hole in the centre of this piece, passing the prong of the buckle through, and doubling the leather to the back of the belt. Make a narrow keeper for the belt end, after passing it first through the buckle. This narrow piece is lined and stitched, then joined to form a ring, slipped over the leather before the buckle and before the leather is folded to the back.

Stitching by hand

A tool known as a 'stitch spacer' can be used for making the holes for stitching, otherwise use an unthreaded sewing machine, moving the stitch to the biggest possible. The stitching can be more regularly done with two needles, these being passed through the same hole in opposite directions.

In this way there is an even pull on both threads, and the stitching is alike on both sides. The sewing is greatly simplified if both hands are free, so that both needles can be pushed through at the same time. This can be done where it is possible to place the work between two heavy objects to serve as a clamp. When it is necessary to hold the work in the hands while sewing, the needles must be pushed through one at a time.

Strong thread should be used for sewing. It should be as near as possible in colour to the work. If the thread is slightly waxed, by pulling it through a piece of beeswax, it will make it firmer and less likely to knot during sewing. The best needles to use are those which have around eye large enough to take the thread easily.

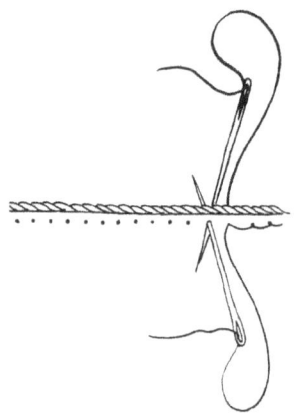

Using two needles for stitching.

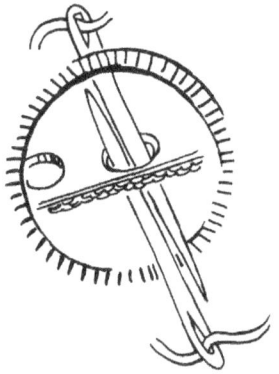

Close-up sketch of two needles.

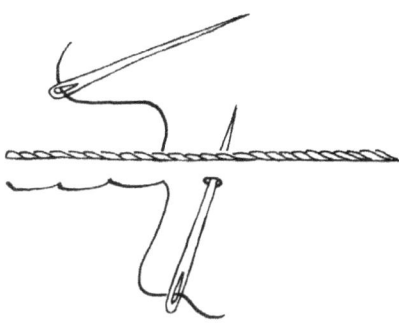

Pushing the needles through one at a time.

If the stitching is done with one needle only, take the needle and thread in and out of the stitch holes, making running stitches. When at the end of the row, turn and come back, in and out, filling up the spaces and making a stitch which resembles machine stitch. Keep the thread pulled taut all the time.

If it is required to hand-stitch with a different colour each side of the work — when, for instance, the edge of your tāniko work may be black, and your leather lining cream — then a needle must be threaded with one colour and the thread fastened on at the beginning of the row.

Withdraw the needle from the thread and re-thread with the second colour. Holding the first thread tightly along the back of the row of holes, stitch with the second colour, taking the needle into each hole in succession, looping the thread over the first colour and returning to the right side of the work. There the second thread must be pulled tightly to draw the first halfway through the thickness of the work.

Construction

Having cut the leather ends of your belt to the required length, sew them to your tāniko work, overlapping the tāniko by about 2.5 centimetres. Glue the lining to the back of your leather, and leave under a weight until thoroughly dry, then stitch along both edges in either of the methods described.

Another way of fastening a lady's belt, instead of using a buckle, is to use two rings. Ordinary brass curtain rings — in a size to suit the width of the belt — are first bound round with macramé twine in one of the colours of your tāniko.

These rings are both slipped over your leather end, the leather is then doubled back so that the rings lie on the fold of the leather, the cut edges then being sewn to the tāniko, overlapping it by about 2.5 centimetres.

The other leather end is pointed, and to fasten is passed through one ring and back through the other, making a very firm form of fastening.

Part 10 Some ornament devices

Most tāniko weavers have not taken the trouble to learn extra techniques that might help in improving the quality and appeal of their work and give it some distinctive features not to be found in the work of any other weaver. It was stressed at the beginning of this book that a good weaver was one who had technical mastery over tāniko; in simple language this means that the weaver should know many techniques and know them better than the average weaver. The aim of this section is to provide some ideas that might prove helpful.

The first point to stress about the extra ornamental devices illustrated here is that none of them is a modern invention. They all belong to the tool kit of the traditional weaver and have all been used many times before, but they are largely unknown to many present-day weavers of tāniko.

Weft ornamental techniques

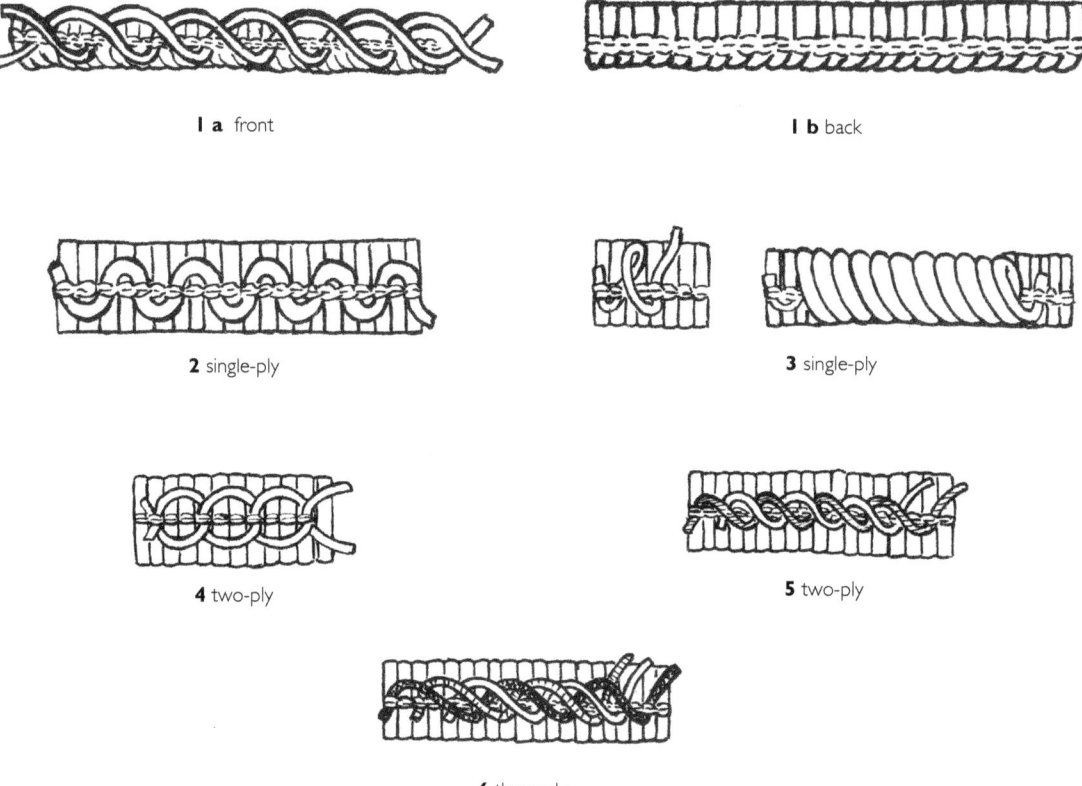

I a front

I b back

2 single-ply

3 single-ply

4 two-ply

5 two-ply

6 three-ply

The first six ornamental ideas presented here may be applied to belts, bodices, headbands, bandoliers and purses, and all are worked in during the casting-on and casting-off stages. These extra ornamental threads may be left loose, such as in 2, 3 and 4, or they may be pulled more tightly as in 1, 5 and 6.

The ideas presented in diagrams 7 to 15 are probably best suited for larger work, such as bodices, baskets and bandoliers. Decorated short tags, round or flat, and dyed in the same way as piupiu strands, are used in 7, 8 and 9. In 10, 11, 12 and 15, dyed pieces of karure (doubled threads of flax fibre) are used. All attachments such as are used in these examples are called hukahuka — ornamental weaving attachments.

Feather attachments are illustrated in diagrams 13 and 14. The final diagram illustrates an idea which can be applied very effectively to bodices, that is, to the bottom border.

Techniques of adding tags, pompoms, feathers and fringes

[Illustrations are after Buck]

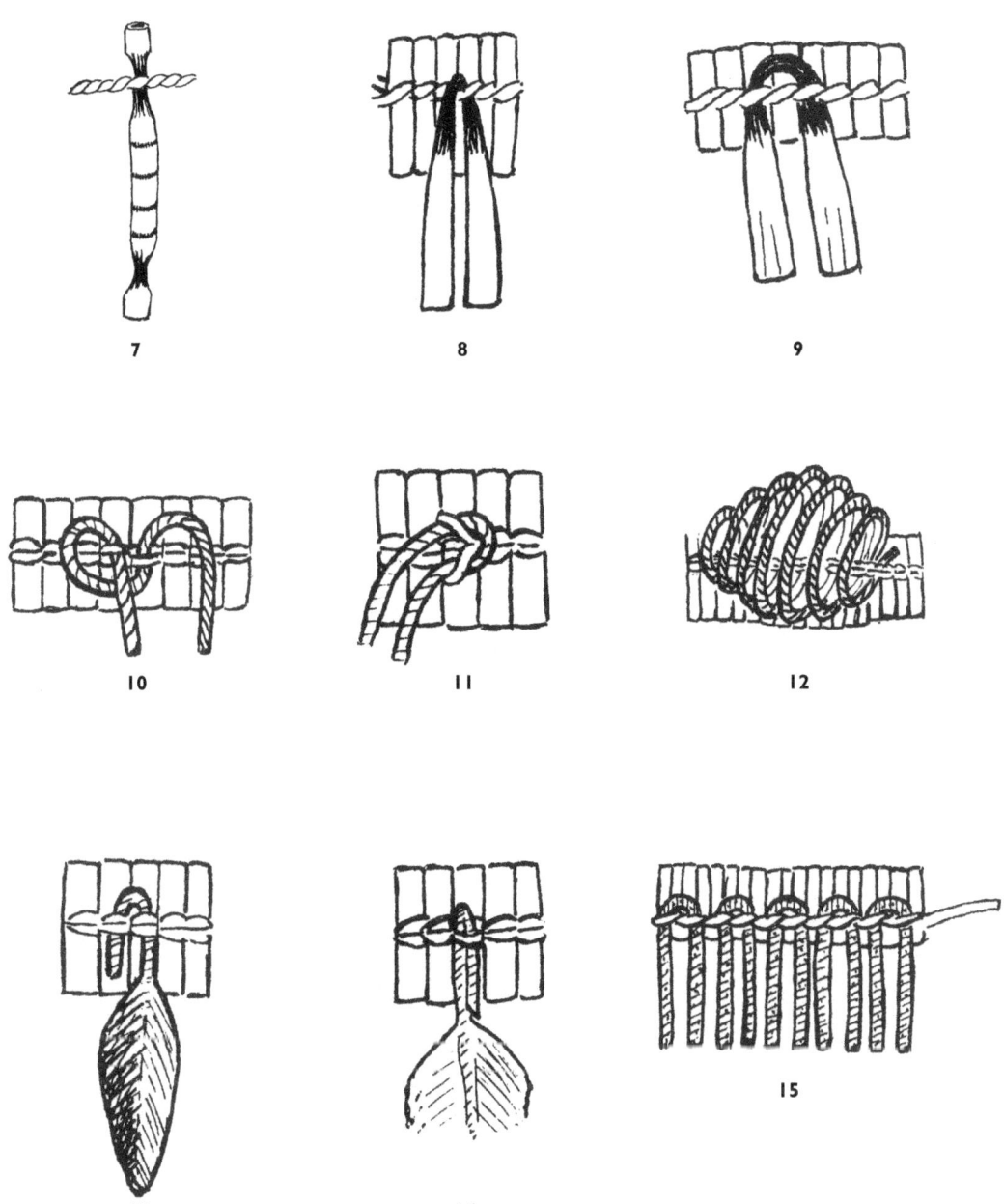

7

8

9

10

11

12

13

14

15

Part 11 Other uses of tāniko weaving

We saw in the first part of this book that tāniko has been applied to cloaks, piupiu, bodices, bandoliers, headbands and belts. Examples of such work have been provided throughout the book. Now, what of other possibilities?

It is largely a matter of imagination. Tāniko has been used in the past to make purses, tobacco pouches, table mats, serviette rings, baskets, handbags, wallets and doily sets. One enterprising male experimenter has tried working tāniko bands into Fair Isle jerseys. Another has used it for the front of a waistcoat, and maybe someone has tried the idea of making neckties in tāniko. In the past hats have been made in tāniko. The technique has been very effectively used in churches for decorating the altar and the pulpit, and in some cases it has been applied to the priest's regalia. Thus, many possibilities are open to any weaver who has sufficient mastery over the technique.

Past weavers have produced many beautiful articles which in their small way contributed to the cultural wealth of New Zealand. What happens to the technique in the future depends largely on practical weavers, on whether they keep it up and find a place for it in this modern world, or whether they allow it to fade peacefully away.

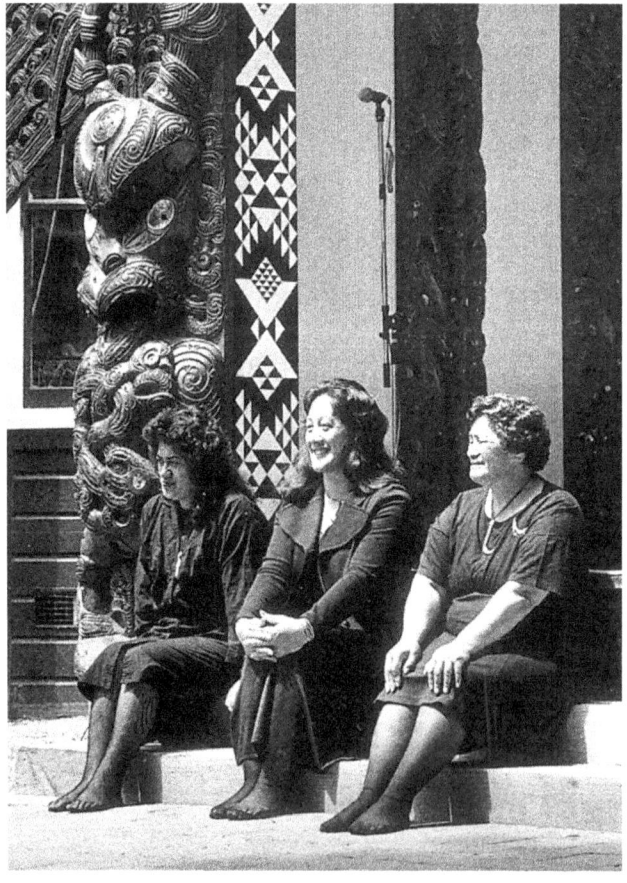

Painted tāniko patterns are often applied to decorated meeting houses. They are shown here painted on the porch of Te Herenga Waka at Victoria University, Wellington, opened 1986.
Photo: Victoria University

Glossary of Māori words

aho (n): weft thread

aho tāhuhu (n): the weft thread strung across the weaving pegs

aho tapu (n): the casting-on thread of the sampler made during initiation

āhua (n): semblance or likeness, the conceptual aspect of an artefact

aonui (n): tāniko patterns based on the triangle motif (also called aronui)

aramoana (n): tāniko patterns based on continuous chevrons without serrations

atiraukawa (n): a variety of flax with fibre of high quality for weaving; the young leaf is bright olive-green which turns a bronze colour when mature

aute (n): paper mulberry tree, *Broussonetia papyrifera*

harakeke (n): New Zealand flax, *Phormium tenax*

hāro (v): to remove the flax fibre from the leaves by cutting across the underside, then drawing over a shell

hautonga (n): south wind

huaki (n): cloak which has double taniko borders along the sides and bottom, and which has horizontal wefts in the woven foundation

hūhi (n): variety of flax with dark edges to the leaves

Hui Tōpu (n): annual Anglican festival for Māori parishes in the eastern part of New Zealand

hukahuka (n): ornamental tags and threads added to the woven foundation

huruhika (n): superior variety of flax

kahu, kākahu (n): general name for Māori cloaks

kahu huruhuru (n) general term for any cloak decorated mainly with feathers

kahu kura (n): cloak decorated with the red feathers of the native parrot, *Nestor meriodianalis*

kahu tūpāpaku (n): any cloak used to drape over a corpse

kaitaka (n): class of cloaks which are decorated with tāniko (also known as parawai)

kanono (n): tree, *Coprosma australis*, used for dyeing

kaokao (n): class of tāniko patterns in which upturned chevrons are used

kāretu (n): sweet-scented grass, *Hierochloe antarctica*, worn as a pubic covering by women in the Classical period

karure (v): to twist two minimal threads to form a double thread; (n): two-ply thread

katau (n): first part of the rolling process in which the threads are rolled forward from the body, down and to the right of the leg

kōhunga (n): superior variety of flax with narrow leaf olive-green in colour with edge and keel fading on the upper side (term is used in the Waikato-Maniapoto area)

kōmiri (v): to rub with the fingers

korowai (n): class of cloaks in which body ornamentation consists of pom poms, tassels, tags and thrums

kōwhaiwhai (n): general name for painted rafter patterns

kumete (n): wooden bowl into which hot stones were placed to boil water

makomako (n): tree, *Aristotelia serrata*

mana (n): prestige, authority, power

Māoritanga (n): concept of Māoriness, of what it means to be Māori

marae (n): village plaza

maramara (n): Wanganui term for the mud used in obtaining a black dye (known also as uku or paru)

marangai (n): east wind, east

matau (n): right

mauī (n): left

miro (n): fine thread used as weft material in weaving

niho, whakaniho (n): teeth or serrations on patterns; (v): to make such serrations

oue (n): superior variety of flax such as the kōhanga

paepaeroa (n): cloak with vertical wefts in the main body and with single tāniko borders along the sides and bottom

paepaeroa-huaki (n): cloak with vertical wefts in the body and double tāniko borders along the side and bottom borders

pakawhā (n): outside dried leaves of a flax plant

Pākehā (n): general term for persons of European descent

pāpaka (n): pattern based on the basket weave that has a perpendicular line through each diamond

parawai (n): Wanganui class name for cloaks decorated with tāniko

pare (n): headband (also tipare)

pari (n): bodice used during ceremonials

pātea (n): cloak in which body wefts are horizontal, and the sides and bottom borders have single tāniko bands

pātere (n): abusive song

pātikitiki (n): term coined for patterns based on single diamonds

pātikitiki-papaki-rango (n): East Coast term for patterns based on the basket weave

patu muka (n): stone pounder used for beating flax fibre

patu whitau (n): another name for a stone beater

pauku, pukupuku (n): war cloak made entirely of the close single-pair twine, and worn as protection against spear thrusts

piupiu (n): kilt worn by male and female performers during ceremonial occasions and concerts

poi (n): light ball with short or long string attached that is swung and twirled in native dances

pūahi (n): type of dogskin cloak in which the foundation was covered with strips of white, hairless dogskin

pungarehu (n): ashes

rāpaki (n): garment, usually a cloak, worn around the waist

raukūmara (n): tāniko patterns composed mainly of horizontal and vertical lines

raurēkau (n): tree of the Coprosma family

rei puta (n): whalebone neck pendant popular in the Classical period

rongo tainui (n): superior variety of flax

rukutia (n): superior variety of flax

takikau (n): variety of flax from which high-grade fibre can be drawn without the use of shell

takiri (n): jerking technique used to strip fibre away from the flax leaves; (v): to do the above

tānekaha (n): tree, *Phyllocladus*

tangi (n): mourning ceremony performed over the dead; (v): to mourn or weep

tāniko (n): weaving technique to produce patterns; (v): to perform the technique

tapa (n): cloth beaten from the paper mulberry tree

tāpeka (n): patterned bandolier worn by males as ceremonial costume

tapu (a): under religious restriction; (n): condition of being under religious restriction

taupokipoki (n): pattern of simple alternating triangles

tawatawa (n): pattern based on vertical and horizontal lines

tihoi (n): extra wefts inserted in the body of garments to allow for body fit; superior variety of flax

tīhore (v): to peel, strip or remove the skin; (n): superior variety of flax in which the fibre is easily removed

tiki (n): greenstone neck ornament

toatoa (n): tree, *Phyllocladus tricomanoides*

tukemata (n): class of patterns based on serrated chevrons

tukutuku (n): lattice-work used in the decoration of superior houses

turuturu (n): pegs used by weavers to hold their work in place

tutu (n): shrub, *Coriaria arborea*, the bark of which was used as a dye mordant

uku (n): rusty-coloured mud used to obtain a black dye

waharua (n): class of patterns based on two or more diamonds placed one above the other (literally, two mouths)

waitumu (n): mordant used in dyeing flax

whakaio (v): to separate prepared fibre in to hanks

whakamaroke (v): to dry, to cause to dry

whakarua kōpito (n): class of patterns, the same as waharua

whenu (n): warp thread

whīnau (n): tree, *Elaeocarpus dentatus*, the bark of which was used as a dye (also known as hinau)

whitau (n): high-grade prepared flax fibre

Bibliography

Adam, L., *Primitive Art*. Allen Lane Penguin Books, Middlesex, 1940.

Angas, George French, *The New Zealanders Illustrated*, Thomas Mclean, London, 1846.

Angas, George French, *Savage Life and Scenes: Being an Artist's Impression of Countries and Peoples of the Antipodes*, Smith, Elder & Co., London, 1847.

Barrow, Terence, *'Taniko Weaving of the New Zealand Maori'*, Palette, No. 9, Spring,1962.

Beaglehole, J. C. (ed.), *Journals of Captain James Cook on his Voyages of Discovery*, 2 vols, Cambridge University Press, 1955.

Beaglehole, J.C., *The Endeavour journal of Joseph Banks*, 2 vols, Angus and Robertson, Sydney, 1962.

Best, Elsdon, *'The Art of the Whare Pora'*, *Transactions of the N.Z. Institute, Vol. XXXI*, pp. 625-58, 1898.

Best, Elsdon, *The Maori*, 2 vols, Memoir of the Polynesian Society, 1941.

Boas, Franz, *Primitive Art*, Dover Publications Inc., New York, 1955.

Buck, Sir Peter (Te Rangi Hiroa), *'On the Maori Art of Weaving Cloaks, Capes, and Kilts'*, *New Zealand Dominion Museum Bulletin, No. 3*, pp. 69-90, 1911.

Buck, Sir Peter, *'Maori Plaited Basketry and Plaitwork'*, Transactions of N.Z. Institute, Vol. 54, p. 705-4 2, 1923.

Buck, Sir Peter, *The Evolution of Maori Clothing*, Memoir of the Polynesian Society,1926.

Department of Maori Affairs, *Te Ao Hou, The New World*, Wellington.

Flax Commission Report 1871, in Appendices to the Journal of the House of Representatives, Vol. 11, G -4, Government Printer, Wellington.

Gerbrands, A. A., *Art as an Element of Culture, Especially in Negro Africa*, Mededelingen van het Rijksmuseum voor Volkenkunden, No. 12, Leiden, 1957.

Green, Roger C., *A Review of the Prehistoric Sequence in the Auckland Province*, N.Z. Archaeological Association, Auckland, 1963.

Hamilton, Augustus, *Maori Art: The Artworkmanship of the Maori Race in New Zealand*, Ferguson & Mitchell, Dunedin ,1901.

Kroeber, A. L., *Style and Civilizations*, University of California Press, 1963.

Martin, Paul, S., *'Archaeological Work in the Ackmen-Lowry Area, South western Colorado'*, Anthropological Series, XXIII, No. 2, Field Museum of Natural History,1938.

Mead, S. M., *Taniko Weaving: How to Make Maori Belts and Other Useful Articles*, A.H. & A.W. Reed, Wellington, 1952.

Mead, S. M., *'Technological and Functional Change in Traditional Maori Clothing'*, unpublished thesis, University of Auckland, 1965.

Merriam, Alan P., *The Anthropology of Music*, Northwestern University Press, 1964.

Metge, A. Joan, *A New Maori Migration: Rural and Urban Relations in Northern New Zealand*, Athlone Press, London, 1964.

Osgood, Cornelius, *'Ingalik Material Culture'*, Yale University Publications in Anthropology, No. 22, New Haven, 1940.

Parkinson, Sydney, *A Journal of a Voyage to the South Seas in His Majesty's Ship the 'Endeavour'*, Richardson and Urquhart, 1773.

Phillipps, W.J., *Maori Rafter and Taniko Designs*, Wingfield Press, Wellington, 1960.

Ramsden, Eric, *Sir Apirana Ngata and Maori Culture*, A. H. & A.W. Reed, Wellington,1948.

Roth, H. Ling, *The Maori Mantle*, Bankfield Museum, Halifax, 1923.

Ryden, Stig, *The Banks Collection: An Episode in 18th-Century Anglo-Swedish Relations*, Almqvist & Wiksell, Stockholm, 1963.

Sapir, Edward, *'Fashion'*, in David G. Mandelbaum (ed.), *Selected Writings of Edward Sapir in Language, Culture and Personality*, University of California Press, pp. 373-81, 1949.

Schapiro, Meyer, *'Style'*, in A. L. Kroeber (ed.), *Anthropology Today*, Chicago, pp.287-312, 1953.

Sinclair, Keith, *A History of New Zealand*, Penguin Books Ltd, Middlesex, 1959.

Taylor, Walter W., *A Study of Archaeology*, American Anthropological Association ,1948.

Tregear, Edward, *The Maori People*, A. D. Willis Ltd, Wanganui, 1926.

Williams, Herbert W., *A Dictionary of the Maori Language*, 6th edition, Government Printer, Wellington, 1957.

Wright, Olive (ed. and trans.), *The Voyage of the Astrolabe — 1840: An English Rendering of the journals of Dumont d'Urville and his Officers of their Visit to New Zealand in 1840*, etc., A. H. & A.W. Reed, Wellington ,1955.

Index

adding tags, pom poms, feathers, fringes
    124–25
adoption
    of alien symbolism 55, 64, 75
    of European clothing 54
    of Māori costume as national costume 54
advantages
    of tāniko 35
    of tapestry 58
aho tapu 19, 69–70
āhua 58
Angas, George French 48–50
artefact
    attributes of 57–58
    fundamental aspect 58, 95

bandoliers 12, 17, 47, 56, 64, 66, 124, 126
Banks Collection 34, 73
Banks, Joseph 22, 35–36, 38–40, 61–62
Barrow, Terence 14, 27, 72
belts 6, 12, 18, 22, 38–39, 65–66, 75, 96, 110, 113
    examples of 68, 73, 74, 77
    instruction for making 99–121
    lining of 121–23
Best, Elsdon 24, 26–27
Boas, Franz 13–14, 76, 97
bodices 6, 12–14, 16–17, 46–47, 56, 58, 65–66,
    124, 126
Buck, P. H. (Te Rangi Hiroa) 14, 21, 26–28, 30–32,
    34, 52, 71–73, 98, 105

casting off 111–13
    alternatives 114–16
casting on 19, 77, 100–104
    alternatives 114–16
ceremonial costume 6–7, 11–18, 46–47, 51–54
change
    in aesthetic conventions 48–50
    in costume 11–12
    in fashions 54–56
    in techniques 50–51, 56–57
Christian influence 16, 55, 60, 64
Classical Māori period 14, 17, 36–45, 48, 54–55,
    60–61, 63–67, 70, 72, 94–96, 110
classification of patterns
    Barrow's types 72
    Buck's system 72–73
    general 71–93
    Phillipps' addition to system 72–73
cloak types
    dogskin 30, 32, 34–35, 39–41, 47, 49
    huaki 40, 42–43
    kahu huhuhuru 48–49
    kahu kura 39
    kaitaka 28, 39–43, 47–50, 54
    korowai 39, 48–49, 51, 54
    paepaeroa 21, 26, 41–43
    paepaeroa-huaki 43
    pātea 37, 42–43
    pūahi 32, 34–35
    pukupuku 32

cloaks to cover coffins 54
clothing
    Classical Māori period 36–44
    introduction of European clothing 45
    maximum 39–40
    minimum 39
    Modern period 51–57
    Transitional period 44–51
colour
    dyeing process 26–29
    four-colour patterns 82–83, 86–87
    general 19, 26–29, 47
    three-colour patterns 78–79, 81–83,
    86–89, 91
    two-colour patterns 78–82, 84–86, 88,
    90–91
commencement methods
    paepaeroa cloaks 43
    selvedge 30–31
    tāniko 30–31, 101–104
    thrum 30
conservative weavers 60, 66–68, 95–96
Cook, James 17–18, 22, 33, 36, 38–39, 44, 60–61,
    63, 94
Coronation celebrations at Ngaruawahia 11, 53
costume for mourning 54
cultural context 11–18

development of tāniko 36–58
downward weaving 12, 19, 21
d'Urville, Jules Dumont 45–46
dyeing
    black dye 26–27
    flax fibre 26–27
    red dye 27
    ritual of 28–29
    yellow dye 27

fashion
    Classical Māori period 37–44
    in ceremonial costume 51–54
    Modern period 52, 54–58
    Transitional period 45–51
feathers 12, 15, 17–18, 26, 39–41, 47, 49–50, 54,
    96, 124–125
finger weaving 7, 12, 21, 96
Flax Commission 22

flax (harakeke, *Phormium tenax*) 12, 22, 45
    beating of fibre 22, 24
    cutting strands 22
    drying 24
    hanking 24
    rolling into fibre 24–26
    stripping by hāro method 23–24
    stripping by takiri method 24
    washing 24, 28
flax varieties 22
free-for-all weavers 66

girdles 38–39
graphed patterns 78–93
graphing a pattern 99–101

harakeke — see flax
hāro method 23–24
headbands 12, 17, 56, 65–66, 124, 126
Hui Tōpu 11
hurihanga takapau ritual 69–70

influence
    of Christianity 16, 55, 60, 64
    of ministerial visits 11, 67
    of royal and vice-regal visits 11, 67
initiation ceremony 69–70

katau movement 25–26
Kroeber, A.L. 51, 97

lining and finishing 16, 121–23

Māori costume 11–18
Māori culture groups 11–13, 15–16
Māoritanga 98
Martin, Paul S. 58
mauī movement 26
Merriam, Alan P. 95
motor habits 32–33

ornamental devices 123–125
Osgood, C. 58

paper mulberry 22, 38
Parkinson, Sydney 31
passive threads 19–21, 110–11

pattern names
    aramoana 65, 71–72, 74, 76, 78
    kaokao 89
    kōwhaiwhai 90
    pāpaka 85
    pātikitiki-papaki-rango 14, 76, 84
    raukūmara 88
    taupokipoki 79
    tawatawa 88
    whakaniho 80
pattern types
    aonui or aronui 65, 71–72, 74, 79–82
    based on horizontal and vertical lines
        (raukūmara) 88
    based on representational motifs 75,
        92–93
    based on scroll (kōwhaiwhai) 75, 90–91
    pātikitiki 75, 82–85
    tukemata 65, 71–72, 74, 78–79
    waharua 65, 75, 86–87
    whakarua kōpito 65, 71–72, 75, 86–87
patterns
    classification of 14, 59, 71–93
    graphed 78–93
    naming of 76
    negative aspect 75
    positive aspect 75
penis string 39
Phillipps, W. J. 14, 72
piupiu (kilt) 6, 15–16, 39, 47, 49, 54–56, 97, 124,
    126
poi 6, 11
position one 33, 107–109
position two 33, 107–109
preparing a pattern 99–101
preparing warps and wefts 101

rāpaki 39
revival of Māori art 53, 66
ritual
    dyeing operations 26–29
    tohi 69–70
    turning the floor mat 69
rolling fibre
    karure 26, 124
    miro 26
Roth, Ling 20, 61

royal visits 11, 53
Ryden, Stig 34–35, 61

sacred peg (turuturu tapu) 69
Schapiro, Meyer 59, 97
shark teeth pendants 12, 17–18, 40
simplification
    in cloak design 54
    in piupiu 55
social change 44–47
specialisation in weaving 12–13
style
    changes 58, 70, 94–98
    conservative aspect 60
    continuity of 71–73
    definition 59–60
    development 59–60
    fragmentation of 64, 94–96
    general 59–70, 94–98
    group style 60
    influence of society 60–61
    splitting 65–67, 95–96
    tradition 60–61
superstition
    in dyeing 28
    in weaving 69–70
symbolism in cloaks 54
takiri method of stripping 24
tāniko
    borders on dogskin cloaks 30
    definition 12, 19
    development from basketry 35
    development from dogskin cloaks 34
    discovery of 30–35
    materials 19–20
    method of holding 33–34
    technique 19–20
    twisting 20
    uses of 126
    weave 105–120
tapa cloth 22, 38, 40
tapestry technique 6, 13, 15, 17, 35, 50, 56–58, 66,
    95–96
tattoo 7, 12, 15, 17–18, 21, 40, 60
Taylor, Walter 58
technical changes 50–51, 56–57
tiki ornaments 7, 12, 17–18, 40

tohi ritual 69–70
tourist trade 54, 66
tukutuku (lattice-work) 21, 77, 97
turuturu (weaving pegs) 19, 21, 69

weavers
    George, Mrs Dick 13, 68, 74, 76
    Hall, Mrs Rangimakehu 48
    Hetet, Mrs Rangimarie 13, 23, 32, 96–97
    Hohepa, Mr W. 74, and graphed pattern 21
    Mead, Mrs June 77
    Raponi, Mrs Elsie 57
    Stirling, Mrs P., graphed patterns 6, 17, 18, 20

Te Kanawa, Mrs D. 46, 97
Tere, Mrs June 73
Whaipooti, Mrs Anne 74
weaving techniques
    close single-pair twine 31–32
    single-pair twine 30–35
    spaced single-pair twine 31
    tāniko weave 33, 105–120
    two-pair interlocking weft 19, 21, 30
    wrapped twine 21, 34, 105
weft ornamental techniques 124

Young Māori Party 52